Cognitive Cooking
with Chef Watson

Recipes for Innovation from IBM & the Institute of Culinary Education

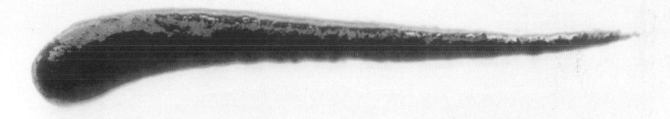

sourcebooks

Copyright © 2015 by IBM Corporation and Institute of Culinary Education, Inc.
Cookbook design by Don Morris, Don Morris Design
Recipe Development and Plating: James Briscione & Michael Laiskonis
Photography and Food Styling: Todd Porter & Diane Cu-Porter
Editor: Pennie Rossini
Icons: Martin Gee
Text: Stephen Baker & Stephen Hamm

Production management by The Stonesong Press, LLC
Sourcebooks and the colophon are registered trademarks of Sourcebooks, Inc.

Published by Sourcebooks, Inc.
P.O. Box 4410, Naperville, Illinois 60567-4410
(630) 961-3900
Fax: (630) 961-2168
www.sourcebooks.com

Library of Congress Cataloging-in-Publication data is on file with the publisher.

Printed and bound in U.S.A. by Walsworth Publishing Company
10 9 8 7 6 5 4 3 2 1

COGNITIVE

C C

COOKING

 IBM

ibm.com/cognitivecooking

Introduction

The ideas for the recipes in this book weren't generated by your average chef. What kind of eccentric would ever dream up a Turkish-Korean Caesar salad or a Cuban lobster bouillabaisse? In this case, it's one that has never tasted a single morsel of food. This culinary prodigy, in fact, has no taste buds, no nose, nor any sensual experience of food or drink.

Chef Watson is a powerful technology. In one sense, it's a tool like many others in the kitchen, such as the meat thermometer and the scale. But while those devices provide simple data on temperature and weight, Watson yields a far richer harvest: creative ideas.

You might wonder why IBM, a company focused on technology for the enterprise, would take this apparent detour into the kitchen. The answer has to do with creativity and discovery. It represents the loftiest realm of cognition. A single new idea, after all, can launch entire companies or industries. It can lead to an artistic masterpiece or fuel a dramatic medical breakthrough. Creativity changes history, and we have always considered it the pinnacle of intelligence and, perhaps, the essence of what it means to be human.

Through the decades, we've farmed out enormous portions of our day-to-day work to computers, but almost all of it has been in the domains of facts and numbers. Blazing through trillions of numbers in a second, computers are wizards at processing petabytes of existing information. But creating something entirely new? That requires a spark of intelligence that only humans can ignite—at least, that's the traditional thinking.

For three years, researchers at IBM focused on building an idea-generating tool. They then teamed up with world-class chefs from the Institute of Culinary Education (ICE) to turn the exotic combinations of ingredients cascading out of the computer into culinary delicacies. This cookbook shows not only how far Watson has come, but also the incredible, untapped potential of further collaborations between man and machine.

This journey at IBM began nearly a decade ago, when a team of researchers set out to create a question answering system to take on human champions in the TV quiz show *Jeopardy!* They named the system Watson, after IBM's first Chairman and CEO, Thomas J. Watson Sr. Its challenge was immense. Competing against human beings with encyclopedic memories and lightning-fast recall, Watson had to make sense of complex clues, sift through a vast trove of books, lists, and articles to find potential answers, and then calculate if it had enough confidence in an answer to place a bet on it. The system worked. Watson triumphed on *Jeopardy!* in early 2011—defeating two former grand champions.

Watson wasn't just a game champion, but the beginning of a new era of computing. Since the 1940s, when the first electronic, programmable computers emerged, these machines have helped to transform business, society, and our personal lives. Yet, until recently, computers were always limited by the fact that humans had to program a detailed set of rules and instructions. Beyond that, they were helpless. But now, thanks to advances in computer science, we're entering the era of cognitive computing, of systems that learn.

Like Watson, future systems in this dawning age will feast on massive amounts of data, much of it in words and images. They will refine this knowledge into insights and use it to provide services and recommendations that feel both timely and intuitive. What's more, through their interactions with us, these systems will adjust to what we're looking for and learn over time.

The Watson seen on *Jeopardy!* showed the world an early prototype of a cognitive system. Even before the legendary televised showdown, IBM researchers were readying its technological offspring for important jobs in everything from health care to financial services. For example, IBM scientists are currently working with some of the world's leading medical institutions to use Watson to help physicians find cures for cancer.

But Mahmoud Nagshineh, one of the leaders in IBM Research, had another idea. How about developing a system that could go beyond answers and, instead, create something entirely new? Suggestions poured in. Many were in the traditional fields of creativity, such as arts, literature, and music. But Lav Varshney, a scientist working on IBM's Smarter Cities initiative, suggested building a system that could innovate in a field that every human being appreciates: food.

Lav pointed out that when it comes to cooking, we humans are limited by what we already know, combinations of ingredients that we inherited through various culinary cultures, whether tomatoes with oregano or ginger with scallions. Great chefs might know and draw upon several thousand of these pairings, but considering the vast universe of available ingredients, the number of all possible combinations must certainly be in the trillions, or beyond. A cognitive computing system focused on food, he believed, could help chefs explore these fresh flavor combinations and co-create surprising, never-before-seen dishes.

Why the "co" in front of create? It was clear from the beginning that no computer system, no matter how advanced, could independently come up with complete, delightful, ready-to-cook recipes. It could roam through hundreds of thousands of recipes, vast databases of food chemical compositions, nutritional information, and cultural preferences, and propose bold, new combinations. But Watson needed partners: talented human beings, complete with minds and palates. Cuisine-savvy technologists had to train the system. Later they would work with professional chefs to choose from the most promising of Watson's proposed ingredients, fine-tuning them into succulent, surprising, and novel recipes.

So commenced the journey that led to Chef Watson and this book. Lav teamed up with a colleague, Florian Pinel, a computer scientist who also has a diploma from New York's prestigious Institute of Culinary Education. Together they embarked on the education of a computational—and creative—virtual chef.

They started by training Watson on tens of thousands of recipes, along with loads of information about the chemical composition of foods. But Watson needed further schooling in three areas. First, it had to master food pairings, the flavors and ingredients that complement each other. Entire tomes lay out what humanity has learned about food pairings over the past few thousand years. Rosemary combines well with potatoes, for example, or olives with gin. By studying recipes and the underlying chemical compounds in each ingredient, Watson learned these pairings.

The system would also benefit from research on how people react to the taste and smell of food—what they find pleasing. In recent decades, scientists have given people different flavor compounds to smell and taste, and then asked them to rate each compound for pleasantness. This has produced quantified rankings of our wide-spread preferences at the molecular level.

Perhaps most important for a discovery program like Chef Watson was the third component: the surprise factor. Without it, the system might churn through millions of ingredients and suggest, say, cooking chicken in a wine stew with potatoes, carrots, and onions. But what good is that when the French already have given the world coq au vin? To create bold, new recipes, Watson had to be programmed to produce combinations not yet tasted. This relentless hunt for novelty would fuel its creativity.

Only talented human chefs, however, could turn those surprising ingredient combinations into wonderful food. And the IBM Watson team quickly turned to ICE to provide two of its best: ICE Director of Culinary Development, James Briscione, and Creative Director, Michael Laiskonis.

When the chefs at ICE first came to work with the Watson system, they were naturally curious—and skeptical—about how a computer could enhance their creativity. That said, IBM's proven track record of creative innovation matched perfectly with the school's mission—to help thousands of passionate students find their culinary voice. Lav and Florian's team gained unprecedented access to ICE's database of proprietary recipes, as well as to the school's chefs, kitchens, students, and staff. As James, Michael, and the ICE staff invested hundreds of hours in experimenting and recipe testing, they provided crucial insight into the ways that the Watson system could evolve to support professional chefs. In the process, this collaboration unleashed a torrent of culinary creativity and, as Lav once imagined, never-before-seen recipes, which are detailed in this book.

Chef Watson's cookbook is just the beginning. Eventually, similar cognitive systems may help people compose unique and tasty recipes tailored to their medical needs, their budget, and their desire to eat local foods. It might help schools and hospitals devise dishes that are more nutritious and pleasing to children's or patients' palates. And, more broadly, there will be new uses for discovery technologies across a wide range of industries and domains—from pharmaceuticals and chemicals to media and the arts.

Welcome to the world of creative computing.

SURPRISE   PLEASANTNESS   SYNERGY

Watson System Metrics

Watson uses three different metrics to analyze the ingredients, rated for surprise, pleasantness and synergy.

Here's how each works:

Surprise. By studying tens of thousands of recipes, Watson gets a statistical sense of combinations that are common. By suggesting ingredients and flavors that are rarely found together, Watson creates the unexpected and rates each dish on its surprise scale.

Pleasantness. Researchers have carried out studies on the flavors that give people pleasure at a molecular level. This is called "hedonic psychophysics." Watson rates each dish for this pleasantness component.

Synergy. Studies indicate that foods sharing common chemical flavor compounds taste good together. Much of Western cooking seeks out these pairings, while some Asian cuisines focus instead on contrasts. Watson provides statistics on the synergy of flavor compounds in each of its recipes.

Welcome to Watson

I learned to cook at a very young age while mastering all the family favorites. My mother, my grandmother, and my aunts all had a hand in my education. To me, it was an exercise in memorization and project management (the engineer in me showed up early!). Even in mastering the annual Thanksgiving meal, it was the challenge of timing the final result and delivering consistently to honor our traditions.

Over time I came to realize that the art of cooking runs much deeper than the process itself. One must develop a feel for the ingredients and an understanding of what flavors will correctly accentuate each meal. While I tried to set my sights on greatness, I ultimately became the producer of family tradition versus culinary excellence and creativity.

When my team approached me to describe a new solution built on our Watson technologies—a "Chef Watson"—my reaction was, *seriously?* A system that can master the challenges that I had struggled with throughout my decades in the kitchen? However, my curiosity overcame my skepticism, and I began to learn the method behind the madness.

To start, the team understood something that I failed to consider: There is chemistry behind cooking and ingredients that predetermine which other ingredients will match appropriately with what is in the mix. That understanding would form the basis of a discovery tool, a tool able to start with various ingredients and pair them up based on the underlying chemistry of the ingredients themselves.

This new tool was first taught the chemistry, then trained on styles of cooking such as Indonesian, French, and Tex-Mex. The user could include or exclude ingredients based on availability, allergies, or simply desire. Our first exploration in the public eye was at South by Southwest, an incredible culture and technology event that occurs annually in Austin, Texas. We showed up full of hope and expectation with our cognitive cooking food truck, parked on a street lot, with our signs for all to see in partnership with the Institute of Culinary Education (ICE).

Our partnership with ICE in New York City added a lot of creativity. The recipes and the results are outstanding, my favorite being the Indonesian Rice Chili Con Carne (page 62) made with broth, lemongrass, and vanilla (you have to have a lot of confidence to serve a new take on chili in Texas!).

Over time, our partnerships have expanded and Chef Watson's capabilities have advanced. The system has been trained on the best practices of the chefs supporting *Bon Appétit*, and of course, the creative and innovative chefs at ICE. Now with each set of ingredients and a dash of creativity, up to 100 different approaches to preparation are presented to the user.

The results can be surprising and delicious, which I hope you will discover from the recipes within this book or, more importantly, from your own culinary explorations using Chef Watson.

Enjoy!

MIKE RHODIN
Senior Vice President,
IBM Watson Group

ICE Innovation

When IBM first contacted us two years ago, we were intrigued—and at first even skeptical—about how a computer could collaborate with our chefs to enhance their creativity. But once we learned about the Watson system and its potential to shape the future of creativity, we knew it was an exceptional opportunity for discovery.

The two chefs that have worked on this project—ICE Director of Culinary Development James Briscione and Creative Director Michael Laiskonis—are among the most innovative and accomplished in the industry. Ever since they teamed up with the IBM researchers in the kitchen, it was clear that the system's suggestions represented a new path in the field of culinary innovation. Watson has the potential to change the way chefs experience the creative process— not just by providing surprising concepts and ingredient pairings, but also by representing the levels of pleasantness and surprise that each hypothetical dish should deliver.

The recipes that ICE chefs have been able to develop with the Watson outputs are remarkable, and these dishes are not only pleasing to the eyes and the palate, but stimulate the mind as well.

Our chefs' successes with cognitive cooking are markers of tangible progress and purposeful innovation that transcend novelty or trends—and that is a future for food about which we could not be more excited.

We believe this cookbook is an unprecedented feat, one that will inspire generations of chefs and home cooks to re-think the way we cook and create in the kitchen.

Cheers,

RICK SMILOW
President
Institute of Culinary Education

Meet the Chefs

JAMES BRISCIONE
Director of Culinary Development,
Institute of Culinary Education

James began his culinary adventures as a dishwasher at a brunch restaurant on Pensacola Beach in Florida and never looked back. Passing up a college football scholarship to spend more time in the kitchen, he worked his way up the line at Alabama's Highlands Bar & Grill under James Beard award-winning chef Frank Stitt, achieving the rank of chef de cuisine at the incredible age of 23. During his tenure at Highlands, the restaurant reigned as *Gourmet* magazine's #5 restaurant in the nation. From there, James took on New York City as the sous chef in Daniel Boulud's private dining room at Daniel. Since joining the School of Culinary Arts faculty at ICE, James has become a nationally recognized expert in sous vide and other modernist cooking techniques. Among his various media appearances, James is known for becoming the first-ever two-time *Chopped* champion.

MICHAEL LAISKONIS
Creative Director,
Institute of Culinary Education

Michael joined ICE in 2012 fresh off of an eight-year tenure as Executive Pastry Chef at Le Bernardin. He has long been one of the industry's most creative and talented chefs, noted for having helped Chef Eric Ripert earn three Michelin stars and four stars from the *New York Times*. Best known for his use of modern techniques to reinvent classic desserts, Michael has received numerous accolades, most notably *Bon Appétit*'s 2004 Pastry Chef of the Year and the coveted James Beard Award for Outstanding Pastry Chef in 2007. Most recently, he received the International Association of Culinary Professionals' 2014 Culinary Professional of the Year Award, one of the most distinguished honors in the industry. Outside the kitchen, Michael has also found great success as a writer for publications including *Gourmet*, *Saveur*, and *The Atlantic,* and has appeared on such television shows as *Top Chef: Just Desserts.*

FLORIAN PINEL
Senior Software Engineer,
IBM Watson Group

Florian received a M.S. in Computer Science and Engineering from École Centrale de Paris in France, and a Culinary Arts diploma from the Institute of Culinary Education in New York. Before joining the Watson Group, Florian worked at the IBM T.J. Watson Research Center for fifteen years, focusing on business process management, IT services management, and software as a service. His current research interests are computational creativity and cognitive computing, and he is the lead architect of the Chef Watson project.

1 Chef Watson's First Dishes

In early 2013, Chef Watson made its debut by scouring its vast database and proposing a pastry—the Spanish Almond Crescent. It featured these ingredients:

pepper (spice)	cocoa
saffron	lemon extract
honey	almond
yeast	pastry flour
egg	heavy cream
coconut milk	oil

This list, like others you will see throughout this book, is known as Watson's output. Based on Watson's analysis, each unique combination should produce a flavorful and surprising result. But the computer's output for the almond pastry came without a vision for the finished dish. Figuring out how to combine the ingredients was a challenge that required the expertise of a chef.

The Spanish Almond Crescent was the first of Watson's co-productions with the Institute of Culinary Education and Chef James Briscione. Somehow, Briscione had to turn the unlikely ingredient list into a pastry that not only held together, but also tasted great.

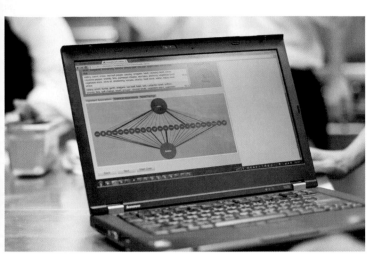

Making a viable pastry dough was the first challenge. The ingredient list was brimming with liquids. It had oil instead of butter and honey, not sugar. It also featured coconut milk and cream. This forced the chef to do research of his own and to innovate. Briscione succeeded in creating a stable dough, but later tests revealed that the recipe looked and tasted even better when he veered from Watson's list and added butter. This is the nature of the human-machine collaboration. The computer doesn't dictate. It suggests.

Following the success of the crescent, the chefs at ICE and the Watson team concocted seven more delicious dishes to serve at an event for financial analysts in San Jose, California. This would be Chef Watson's coming-out party.

Turkish Bruschetta

This recipe was originally topped with a simple preparation of shredded, marinated carrots. I later upped the ante and created spiced carrot pearls. Either way, the result is delicious. Sumac lends a gentle sour note to balance the rich spice in this dish.

CHEF WATSON SAYS

SURPRISE   PLEASANTNESS   SYNERGY

Pro Notes and Tips

- Forming the pearls takes a little practice, but once you get the hang of it, you can make pearls from anything you would like!

EGGPLANT PUREE

2.2	pounds (1,000 grams) Japanese eggplants
1	bunch scallion (60 grams), roots and green tops trimmed
1	tablespoon (8 grams) sumac
½	teaspoon (1 gram) dry oregano
2	teaspoons (7 grams) paprika
1.5	ounces (45 grams) Parmesan cheese
2	teaspoons (10 grams) sunflower oil
1	tablespoon (6 grams) chiffonade basil
2	teaspoons (4 grams) salt

1. Char the eggplants on a flame until black on all sides, then roast at 350°F (175°C) until tender.

2. Cook the scallions on a grill until charred on all sides.

3. Split the eggplants, and scoop the flesh out of the eggplant with a spoon, keeping only a little bit of charred skin. You should have about 1 pound (450 grams) of flesh. Add the sumac, dry oregano, paprika, and Parmesan.

4. Sauté in oil over very high heat for 1 minute, stirring constantly, then transfer to the bowl of a food processor. Add the basil and salt. Blend until smooth.

CARROT PEARLS

2	cups (454 grams) carrot juice
2	teaspoons (4 grams) cumin
1	tablespoon (8 grams) sumac
1	teaspoon (3 grams) salt
1½	teaspoons (5 grams) agar
	bowl of vegetable oil, set over ice

1. Combine the carrot juice, cumin, sumac, and salt in a pot. Bring the mixture to a simmer and cook 2 to 3 minutes to develop the flavors. Remove from the heat and cool completely. Strain the carrot juice into a clean pot.

2. Whisk in the agar until dissolved and return the pot to heat. Cook, stirring gently with a spatula, until the mixture comes to a simmer.

3. Remove the pot from heat and continue stirring until cooled slightly. Transfer the mixture to a squeeze bottle and slowly drip the carrot juice into the ice cold oil to form pearls. When they are all formed, drain the pearls from the oil and rinse in cold water.

TO SERVE

24	thin slices of baguette
	sunflower oil, as needed

1. Drizzle sunflower oil over the bread and toast until crispy.

2. Spread the eggplant puree on the bread slices, then finish with the carrot pearls.

Austrian Grilled Asparagus

Scrolling through possible combinations for a new asparagus dish, there was no need to look any further than the line that contained "pig's feet." This is one of my all-time favorite ingredients, and I was sure it could turn into a winning combination. With the addition of mustard and a mix of Indian spices, an incredible new dish was born.

CHEF WATSON SAYS

SURPRISE

PLEASANTNESS

SYNERGY

Pro Notes and Tips

- You could easily substitute any meat into this recipe—perhaps pork belly or shoulder, or even chicken thighs (with a shortened cooking time).

- If you don't have access to sous vide equipment, brine the meat as directed in the recipe, then remove from liquid and slow cook in a 325°F (160°C) oven in a covered pan until completely tender.

- Or, try it as a vegetarian dish by excluding the meat altogether.

PIG'S FEET SOUS VIDE

2	cups (450 grams) water
1	tablespoon (18 grams) whole grain mustard
1½	tablespoons (15 grams) garlic, minced
1	tablespoon (5 grams) mustard seeds
1	tablespoon (5 grams) fenugreek
2	tablespoons (32 grams) white wine vinegar
2	tablespoons (18 grams) salt
1	tablespoon (15 grams) sugar
2	pig's feet

1. In a bowl, mix the water, whole-grain mustard, garlic, mustard seeds, fenugreek, vinegar, salt, and sugar.

2. Place the marinade and the pig's feet into a sous vide pouch. Seal and refrigerate overnight.

3. Cook the pig's feet in a 162°F (72°C) water bath for 24 hours.

4. Take the feet out of the pouch. Remove the bones and chop the meat, discarding any bits of tough connective tissue or cartilage. Reserve the strained cooking liquid from the pouch.

PIG'S FEET CROQUETTES

6	cups (1,360 grams) water
1	tablespoon (9 grams) salt
2	Idaho potatoes (each 370 grams), peeled, and chopped
1	teaspoon (4 grams) brown mustard seeds
½	teaspoon (2 grams) fenugreek seeds
1	tablespoon (15 grams) canola oil
2	cloves garlic, minced
1	cup (225 grams) pig's feet meat, minced
½	cup (60 grams) Swiss cheese, grated
	all purpose flour, as needed
1	egg, beaten
	potato flakes or panko bread crumbs, as needed

1. Combine the water, salt, and potatoes in a saucepot. Bring to a simmer and cook until the pieces are easily pierced with the tip of a paring knife.

2. Drain the potatoes, then let rest for 30 minutes.

3. Heat the mustard and fenugreek seeds with the oil in a small saucepan over low heat for 2 minutes.

4. Add the garlic and sauté over medium heat for 1 minute. Add the pig's feet and cook for 2 minutes, stirring regularly. Let cool.

5. Rice the potatoes in a bowl and mix in the cheese.

6. Take a quarter of the potatoes and shape into a flat patty. Place some of the meat mixture in the middle, then roll into a log 4 inches long by 1 inch in diameter (10- by 2½-centimeters). Repeat until you have 4 logs.

7. Refrigerate the croquettes for at least 1 hour. Pass them through a standard breading procedure, rolling the croquette in flour, then dipping it in the egg, and finally coating in bread crumbs/potato flakes. Deep-fry at 350°F (175°C) until golden brown.

SPINACH COULIS
    2 cloves garlic, minced
    1 teaspoon (4 grams) canola oil
    1 cup (100 grams) packed spinach
    ½ cup (100 grams) low fat milk
       pinch salt

1. Sauté the garlic in the oil in a pan over medium heat for about 1 minute. Add the spinach and cook for 2 minutes, stirring constantly.

2. Add the milk and salt, and simmer for about 5 minutes.

3. Blend and process until smooth. Reserve, and keep warm.

MUSTARD FOAM
    ½ cup (100 grams) low-fat milk
    2 tablespoons (28 grams) Dijon mustard

1. Heat the milk and mustard in a saucepan for 2 minutes, stirring constantly. Reserve.

GRILLED ASPARAGUS
    12 large spears asparagus, stems trimmed
    1 tablespoon (15 grams) canola oil

1. Bring a large pot of salted water to a boil. Add the asparagus and blanch until halfway done.

2. Drain the asparagus, drizzle with the oil and cook on a hot grill until done and nicely charred.

3. Remove from the heat and plate immediately.

TO SERVE

1. Transfer the mustard foam to a blender and process on high speed until foamy.

2. On each plate, spread a small amount of spinach coulis. Place 3 asparagus spears in the center and 2 croquette halves on the side. Top with the mustard foam.

Indian Turmeric Paella

This recipe brings simple Indian flavors to a classic paella preparation. While Chef Watson didn't suggest adding any seafood to this particular dish, I can imagine that shrimp and/or mussels would be most welcome. Take care when toasting the spices in each step, as this is the key to optimal flavor in the finished dish.

CHEF WATSON SAYS

SURPRISE   PLEASANTNESS   SYNERGY

Pro Notes and Tips

- The crispy layer of rice that forms on the bottom of the pan is called "socarrat," and is always the part everyone fights over. To achieve it, continue cooking after all the liquid has been absorbed to crisp the rice, but keep a careful eye and the heat low to avoid scorching it.

SMOKED HAM HOCK STOCK

1	pound (500 grams) smoked ham hocks
1	pound (500 grams) beef chuck, cubed, and seared
1	quart (1,000 grams) vegetable stock
2	sprigs (6 grams) fresh mint
2	branches (30 grams) fennel greens

1. Place the ham hocks, chuck, vegetable stock, mint, and fennel greens in a pressure cooker. Bring to pressure over medium heat and cook for 1 hour.

2. Strain the stock and reserve.

3. Remove the skin and bones from the ham hocks, cut the meat into chunks, and reserve. Pull the beef into large pieces—do not shred—and reserve.

PAELLA

¼	cup (50 grams) clarified butter
10	cardamom pods
1	branch (2 grams) fresh curry leaves
1	cup (165 grams) Idaho potato, diced
1	whole (65 grams) poblano pepper, diced
1	cup (115 grams) fennel bulb, diced
5	cloves (20 grams) garlic, chopped
2½	cups (450 grams) bomba or arborio rice
1	teaspoon (3 grams) turmeric
1	tablespoon (8 grams) curry powder
½	teaspoon (1 gram) nutmeg, grated
¼	cup (50 grams) light rum
1¼	cups (300 grams) ham hock stock
2½	cups (600 grams) vegetable stock
	kosher salt, as needed
	cherry tomatoes, halved, for garnish

1. Heat the butter in a paella or large nonstick sauté pan. Add the cardamom and curry leaves. Cook until lightly browned and very aromatic.

2. Add the potatoes and sauté 1 minute. Add the poblano and fennel, sauté 1 minute. Add the garlic and cook.

3. Stir in the rice, turmeric, curry powder, and nutmeg. When the rice is well toasted, deglaze the pan with rum and cook until completely dry.

4. Add the stock and meat. Stir well and season to taste with salt. Bring the mixture to a boil, then reduce the heat and simmer approximately 20 minutes (until all of the liquid has been absorbed and the rice on the bottom of the pan begins to brown).

5. To serve, top the paella pan with the cherry tomatoes, green mango salad and fried spinach (recipes to follow).

GREEN MANGO SALAD

½ green mango (100 grams), julienned
2 teaspoons (10 grams) lime juice
2 tablespoons (20 grams) green anaheim chile, thinly sliced
1 tablespoon (10 grams) fresh mint, chopped
kosher salt, as needed

1. Combine the mango, lime juice, chile, and mint. Mix well and season to taste with salt.

CRISP SPINACH

1 cup vegetable oil
1 cup baby spinach

1. Heat the oil in a sauté pan to 350°F (175°C). Add the spinach and cook, stirring gently until crisp. Remove immediately and drain on paper towels.

Italian Grilled Lobster

The original output for this recipe was desperately lacking in acidity, a problem we often ran into early on with Chef Watson. Despite suggesting delicious combinations, outputs occasionally missed on the basic elements of taste, sometimes requiring us to add acidity or spice to balance. I have compensated here by boosting the flavor with white wine vinegar.

CHEF WATSON SAYS

SURPRISE   PLEASANTNESS   SYNERGY

Pro Notes and Tips

• Fregula is a unique pasta from Sardinia, Italy. Made from semolina flour, the dough is rolled into small balls and roasted before cooking.

• If you cannot locate fregula, Israeli couscous is a perfect substitute.

SAFFRON TOMATO SAUCE
  2 tablespoons (28 grams) olive oil
  1 teaspoon (2 grams) dried oregano
     pinch saffron
 15 ounces (425 grams) canned tomatoes, coarsely chopped
  2 tablespoons (25 grams) white wine
     salt and pepper, as needed

1. Place the olive oil, oregano, and saffron in a saucepan over low heat. Let infuse for 4 minutes. Add the white wine and reduce by half.

2. Stir in the tomatoes and gently simmer for 15 minutes. Season to taste with salt and pepper.

3. Blend the mixture with a hand blender. Reserve in a warm place for plating.

ROASTED PUMPKIN
  2 cups (300 grams) pumpkin flesh, small-diced
  1 tablespoon (3 grams) fresh mint, cut into chiffonade
  1 tablespoon (15 grams) olive oil
  1 teaspoon (4 grams) kosher salt

1. Place the pumpkin into an oven-safe dish, then toss with the mint and olive oil.

2. Season with salt, then cook in a 350°F (175°C) oven until tender (about 15 minutes).

LOBSTER FABRICATION
  4 lobsters, each about 1½ pounds (700 grams)

1. Separate the heads, tails, and claws of the lobsters. Keep the heads for another recipe.

2. Bring a pot of salted water to a boil. Blanch the tails for 1 minute and the claws for 4 minutes.

3. Transfer the tails and claws to a bowl of ice water, and let cool.

4. Shell the tails and then lightly score underneath so they stay flat. Reserve.

5. Shell the claws and chop the lobster meat into medium-size chunks. Reserve.

LOBSTER SALAD

- ½ pound dry fregula
  zest of ½ orange
- ½ cup (50 grams) Sicilian green olives, sliced lengthwise
- 2 tablespoons (28 grams) olive oil
- 2 tablespoons orange juice
- 2 teaspoons (10 grams) white wine vinegar
  pinch red pepper flakes
- ½ tablespoon (2 grams) fresh mint, cut into chiffonade

1. Cook the fregula in salted boiling water until tender. Drain and let cool. Measure 1 cup (45 grams) of cooked pasta and reserve the rest for use in another recipe.

2. In a bowl, combine the cooked pasta and the prepared roasted pumpkin, along with the orange zest, green olives, olive oil, orange juice, and white wine vinegar. Mix well and season to taste with salt and pepper.

3. Add the prepared lobster claw meat, red pepper flakes, and mint. Toss again and reserve at room temperature.

GRILLED LOBSTER TAILS

- 6 strips bacon, each 12 inches (30 centimeters) long
- 2 tablespoons olive oil

1. Wrap the reserved lobster tails in bacon and brush each with the olive oil.

2. Cook the tails on a grill over medium heat until well browned on all sides. If the bacon begins to burn on the grill, finish cooking on a rack in the oven. Let rest 2 minutes before slicing.

TO SERVE

- 8 red and yellow cherry tomatoes, halved
  salt, as needed
- 2 tablespoons olive oil

1. Reheat the tomato sauce over low heat.

2. Season the cherry tomatoes with salt.

3. Slice the lobster tails into rounds.

4. On each plate, spread a small amount of the tomato sauce, then arrange a lobster tail and some lobster salad in the center. Decorate with the cherry tomatoes and drizzle with olive oil.

Scandinavian Salmon Quiche

This output may offer relatively few surprises, but instead, it illustrates how Watson uses shared chemical compounds to reinforce what we already know about flavor pairings.

—MICHAEL LAISKONIS

Pro Notes and Tips

• Pasta frolla is a favorite dough in my repertoire, adaptable for both sweet and savory applications. It employs a "mealy" mixing method, cutting the cold butter into the dry ingredients and mixing just until combined.

• The dough, salmon, tomatoes, and mushrooms can be prepared the day before.

PASTA FROLLA

- 2½ cups (300 grams) all purpose flour
- ½ teaspoon (2 grams) fine sea salt
- ¼ cup (50 grams) granulated sugar
- 1 teaspoon (5 grams) baking powder
- ½ cup (12 grams) unsalted butter, cold, cut into small cubes
- 2 eggs (about 100 grams)

all purpose flour, as needed for rolling

butter, as needed for greasing ring molds

1. Thoroughly combine the flour, salt, sugar, and baking powder in the bowl of an electric stand mixer fitted with a paddle attachment.

2. Add the butter and mix on low speed until the mixture resembles coarse cornmeal. The mixture should remain cool and powdery.

3. Add the eggs and continue mixing just until a homogenous dough is formed, taking care not to overwork the dough.

4. Form the dough into a flat square and wrap in plastic film. Chill for 1 hour.

5. Divide the dough in half (reserve the other half in the freezer for future use) and roll to a thin square on a flat, flour-dusted work surface measuring 12- by 12-inches (30- by 30-centimeters) and about ¼-inch (4-millimeter) thick.

6. Cut from the dough 2 circles measuring 8 inches (18 centimeters) in diameter and carefully line 6-inch (15-centimeter) tart rings. Arrange the rings on a parchment-lined sheet pan.

7. Blind-bake the tarts in a preheated 300°F (150°C) oven for 15 to 20 minutes (just until the tart shells turn a light golden brown). Remove from the oven and cool completely.

MAKES 2 TART RINGS ABOUT 6 INCHES (15 CENTIMETERS) IN DIAMETER

 45 MINUTES, PLUS CHILLING, RESTING, AND BAKING

CREATED BY FLORIAN PINEL
REFINED BY MICHAEL LAISKONIS

QUICHE

- 2 plum tomatoes (about 225 grams), thinly sliced
  extra virgin olive oil, as needed
  fine sea salt, to taste
  freshly ground black pepper, to taste
- 2 tablespoons (30 grams) unsalted butter, divided
- 8 ounces (240 grams) salmon filet, cleaned
- 4 medium (100 grams) button mushrooms, sliced
- 4 eggs (200 grams)
- ½ cup plus 2 tablespoons (150 grams) whole milk
- ¼ cup plus 2 tablespoons (80 grams) sour cream
- ½ cup (45 grams) Gruyère, grated, divided
- 1 tablespoon (2 grams) fresh dill, finely chopped, divided
  parsley leaves, as needed

1. Arrange the sliced tomatoes on an oiled sheet pan, lightly season with salt and pepper, and drizzle with an additional spoonful of olive oil. Bake in an oven preheated to 300°F (150°C) for approximately 20 minutes, until partially dried, but not browned.

2. Meanwhile, season the salmon with salt and pepper on both sides, and top with half of the butter. Gently roast in the preheated oven for 15 to 20 minutes. Remove from the oven and, once cooled, carefully flake the salmon into bite-sized pieces.

3. Heat a small sauté pan and lightly brown the mushrooms with the remaining butter over medium heat. Season with salt and pepper. Once browned, remove from the heat and cool.

4. Place the whole eggs in a bowl, whisking to combine. Add the milk, sour cream, and salt to taste. Fold in the cooled salmon, mushrooms, two-thirds of the Gruyère, and half of the chopped dill.

5. Divide the quiche mixture among the baked tart shells (for best results, keep the shells within the tart rings during the baking process).

6. Bake in a preheated 300°F (150°C) oven for 15 to 20 minutes until partially set. Remove and arrange the dried tomato slices atop each quiche, along with the remaining Gruyère. Return to the oven to continue baking for 7 to 10 minutes.

7. Remove the quiches from the oven and cool slightly. Before serving, sprinkle the tops of each with parsley leaves and the remaining chopped dill.

Scandinavian Salmon Quiche

Swiss-Thai Asparagus Quiche

This output presents a few surprising (and perhaps challenging) flavors, particularly with the addition of lemongrass. The combination of dairy products—yogurt, feta, and Gruyère—also serves up an uncommon complexity.

—MICHAEL LAISKONIS

CHEF WATSON SAYS

SURPRISE   PLEASANTNESS   SYNERGY

Pro Notes and Tips

- The pâte croustade formula will make more than is needed for this recipe, but it holds well in the freezer. It is slightly unusual in that the butter is melted, rather than added cold, but the result is a light, flaky dough that is easy to work with.

- The dough, lemongrass infusion, leeks, and asparagus can be prepared a day ahead.

PÂTE CROUSTADE

	scant teaspoon (4 grams) fine sea salt
2½	cups (250 grams) all purpose flour
3	tablespoons (45 grams) warm water
½	cup plus 2 tablespoons (150 grams) unsalted butter, melted
3	egg yolks (60 grams)
	all purpose flour, as needed for rolling
	butter, as needed for greasing ring molds

1. Thoroughly combine the salt and flour in the bowl of an electric stand mixer fitted with a paddle attachment.

2. Separately, stir together the water and butter. Whisk in the egg yolks.

3. Add the liquid mixture to the flour in 3 additions, mixing to produce a homogenous dough (it is normal for the dough to appear slightly rough and greasy at this stage).

4. Form the dough into a flat rectangle and wrap it in plastic film. Chill for 1 hour.

5. Take half of the dough (reserve other half in the freezer for future use) and roll it out on a flat, flour-dusted work surface to create a ⅛-inch (2-millimeter) thick rectangle measuring 8- by 12-inches (20- by 30-centimeters). Transfer the sheet of dough to the refrigerator and let it rest for 20 minutes.

6. Cut 4 circles from the dough, each measuring 5 inches (12 centimeters) in diameter, and carefully line the prepared 4-inch (10-centimeter) tart rings. Arrange the rings on a parchment-lined sheet pan.

7. Blind-bake the tarts in a preheated 320°F (160°C) oven for 12 to 15 minutes, until the tart shells turn a light golden brown. Remove from the oven and cool completely.

QUICHE

½ stalk lemongrass, thinly sliced

1 teaspoon (1 gram) coriander seeds

½ cup (115 grams) whole milk

½ cup (45 grams) leeks, white part only, rinsed and finely chopped

1 tablespoon (15 grams) unsalted butter

fine sea salt, as needed

8-12 thin spears asparagus, woody base of stems removed, and cut into 1-inch (3-centimeter) pieces

water, as needed

3 eggs (150 grams)

1 egg yolk (20 grams)

¼ cup (55 grams) heavy cream

2 tablespoons (30 grams) plain whole milk yogurt

¼ teaspoon (0.5 gram) mild curry powder

freshly ground black pepper, as needed

¼ cup (30 grams) crumbled feta cheese

½ cup (45 grams) Gruyère, grated, divided

1 tablespoon (2 grams) fresh parsley, finely chopped, divided

1. Combine the lemongrass, coriander seeds, and milk in a small saucepan and gently heat to a simmer. Remove from the heat and infuse for 10 to 15 minutes. Strain the milk and cool, discarding the lemongrass and coriander.

2. Meanwhile, heat a small sauté pan and slowly sweat the leeks in the butter, adding salt to taste. Continue to cook until the leeks are soft, but not browned. Remove from the heat and cool.

3. Bring a small saucepan of salted water to a boil. Add the asparagus pieces and blanch for about 30 seconds. Shock asparagus with cold water and drain.

4. Place the whole eggs and egg yolk in a bowl, whisking to combine. Add the infused milk, cream, yogurt, curry powder, black pepper, and additional salt to taste. Fold in the cooled leeks, feta, half of the Gruyère, and half of the chopped parsley.

5. Divide the quiche mixture among the baked tart shells (for best results, keep the shells in the tart rings during the baking process). Add several pieces of asparagus to each quiche and top with the reserved Gruyère.

6. Bake in a preheated 320°F (160°C) oven for 15 to 20 minutes, until set and very lightly browned.

7. Remove the quiches from the oven and cool slightly. Before serving, sprinkle the tops of each with the remaining chopped parsley.

 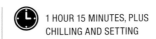

CHEF WATSON SAYS

SURPRISE   PLEASANTNESS   SYNERGY

Spanish Almond Crescent

Crafting the Spanish Almond Crescent was like solving a mystery. Figuring out how to create a pastry with oil, honey, and yeast instead of butter, sugar, and traditional leaveners forced me to dig deep into the traditions and dishes of Spanish cuisine. During my research, I discovered the *xuixo*, a cream-filled pastry typical of the Catalan region. Finding a model for the pastry itself was my first hurdle. Combining saffron, coconut milk, and black pepper into that pastry was my second challenge—one that ended with particularly delicious results.

—JAMES BRISCIONE

Spanish Almond Crescent

HONEY-LEMON DANISH DOUGH

- 2 cups (285 grams) all purpose flour
- 1½ teaspoons (4 grams) fine sea salt
- 1 tablespoon (20 grams) honey
- 1½ teaspoons (5 grams) dry instant yeast
- ¼ cup plus 2 tablespoons (92 grams) whole milk
- 1 tablespoon plus 1 teaspoon (20 grams) coconut milk
- ¼ teaspoon (2 grams) lemon extract
- 2 teaspoons (10 grams) olive oil
- 1 egg (50 grams)
- ½ cup plus 2 tablespoons (150 grams) unsalted butter, softened
- 1 tablespoon (15 grams) olive oil
- all purpose flour, as needed for rolling

1. Place the flour and salt into the bowl of an electric stand mixer, and combine well with the paddle attachment. Add the honey, yeast, milk, coconut milk, lemon extract, oil, and egg. Mix on low until the mass comes together.

2. Increase the mixer speed and continue to work the dough until strong and elastic (about 4 minutes).

3. Cover with plastic wrap and allow the dough to bulk ferment 1 hour at room temperature.

4. Punch down the dough and roll into a rectangle measuring roughly 8- by 16-inches (15- by 30-centimeters). Transfer the dough sheet to a parchment-lined baking pan and refrigerate for a minimum of 12 hours, or up to 24 hours.

5. Combine the softened butter and olive oil, and mix thoroughly to combine. Spread the butter mixture onto a sheet of parchment paper cut to 8- by 8-inches (15- by 15-centimeters), ensuring an even thickness and a clean, square shape. Wrap and chill.

6. To begin the rolling process, place the chilled dough sheet onto a lightly floured work surface and place the butter rectangle over one half of the dough (the rectangle of dough should be roughly twice the size of the butter). Fold the dough over the butter to enclose, and pinch the edges of the dough together.

7. Shift the dough 90° so that the shorter end of the rectangle is facing you and roll the dough in one direction to create a longer rectangle measuring about 8- by 24-inches (20- by 60-centimeters).

8. Brush off any excess flour and fold the rectangle into thirds, as one would fold a letter. This is the first single turn. Place the dough in the refrigerator and allow to rest 30 minutes before rolling and completing the second turn.

9. In the same manner as with the first turn, roll the dough to roughly the same dimensions and fold into thirds a second time. Rest an additional 30 minutes under refrigeration.

10. Complete a third and final turn, also with a 30-minute resting period. At this point the dough can remain in the refrigerator for up to 12 hours.

TO ASSEMBLE

- egg wash, as needed
- saffron pastry cream (recipe follows)
- 3 ounces chopped dark chocolate, or miniature bittersweet chocolate chips
- 1 cup (85 grams) sliced raw almonds
- confectioners sugar, as needed

1. When ready to roll, cut, and shape the pastries, divide the dough in half and roll each portion to a rectangle measuring roughly 9- by 8-inches (24- by 20-centimeters) and just less than ⅜-inch (1-centimeter) thick.

2. Mark 3-inch (8-centimeter) increments along the length of the dough, and 2-inch (5-centimeter) increments along the width to create about 12 rectangles.

3. Lightly brush each rectangle with the egg wash and apply a thin line of the saffron pastry cream and some of the chocolate along one edge and gently roll, leaving the seam on the bottom. Using a sharp knife, cut 4 incisions along one edge and pull the ends together to form a slight U-shape opposite from the side where incisions are.

4. Transfer the shaped pastries to a parchment-lined sheet pan, loosely cover with plastic, and allow to slowly proof at a warm room temperature for 1 to 2 hours (or until nearly doubled in size).

 MAKES 20 TO 24 CRESCENTS

 1½ TO 2 HOURS, PLUS DOUGH RESTING AND PROOFING

 JAMES BRISCIONE AND MICHAEL LAISKONIS

5. When fully proofed, gently brush crescents with the egg wash and top with sliced almonds. Bake in a preheated oven at 350°F (175°C) 15 to 20 minutes, or until a deep golden brown. Remove from the oven and cool.

SAFFRON PASTRY CREAM
1¾ cups (400 grams) coconut milk
   pinch (0.25 gram) saffron
¼ cup plus 2 teaspoons (100 grams) honey
1 teaspoon (2 grams) lemon extract
1 egg
1 egg yolk
⅓ cup (50 grams) pastry flour
   pinch kosher salt
   pinch black pepper

1. Combine the milk, saffron, honey, and lemon oil in a small saucepot and bring to a simmer. Remove from heat and set aside.

2. In a separate bowl, whisk together egg, egg yolk, pastry flour, salt, and pepper.

3. Slowly whisk the hot milk into egg mixture, then return to stove and cook, stirring constantly until thickened. Remove from heat and keep stirring to cool slightly.

GLAZE
1 cup coconut milk
1 tablespoon plus 2 teaspoons honey

1. Combine the coconut milk and honey in a small pan. Bring to a simmer and cook until reduced by half.

Original Dough Recipe (without butter)

1¾ cups (400 grams) coconut milk
1¼ cups (290 grams) heavy cream
3 tablespoons (70 grams) wildflower honey
1 tablespoon (8 grams) yeast
1 egg
3⅓ cups (454 grams) flour
½ teaspoon (1 gram) black pepper

1. Combine the cream and honey in a saucepot and heat to about 100°F. Remove from heat and sprinkle the yeast over the cream. Let stand 1 minute, then whisk to combine. Beat the egg into the mixture.

2. Combine the flour and black pepper in an electric mixer fit with a dough hook. Begin mixing and pour in the liquid ingredients. Mix until the dough forms a tight ball. Let rest 15 minutes.

3. Follow assembly instructions from the previous dough recipe, but do not cut incisions.

4. To cook filled pastries, heat a pot of oil to 350°F. Fry the crescents for approximately 90 to 120 seconds, turning often so that they cook evenly. Remove to a paper towel-lined tray to drain.

Caymanian Plantain Dessert

On the surface, this list of ingredients may not seem all that surprising. The challenge came with framing them in the context of a dessert, especially the plantain, a starchy cousin of the banana that is most common in Latin and Caribbean dishes. This simple approach—frying until crisp—provided a much-needed textural contrast.

—MICHAEL LAISKONIS

CHEF WATSON SAYS

SURPRISE   PLEASANTNESS   SYNERGY

Pro Notes and Tips

- Slice the plantain as thin and as evenly as possible for the crispiest chips.

- If you have leftover lime cream, keep it in the refrigerator for 1 to 2 weeks—it's a great complement for fresh fruit when you want a light dessert.

CARAMELIZED BANANAS

- ½ cup (110 grams) heavy cream (35% fat)
- 3 tablespoons (55 grams) granulated sugar
- 1 tablespoon (25 grams) molasses
  water, as needed
- 2 large bananas (100 grams), peeled, and diced
- 1 tablespoon (15 grams) unsalted butter, softened

1. In a heavy saucepan, combine the cream, 1 tablespoon sugar, and molasses. Bring to a boil. Remove from the heat and reserve.

2. In a second saucepan, carefully cook 2 tablespoons sugar and water to cover over medium heat until it produces a light amber color.

3. Reduce the heat and add the bananas, followed by the cream mixture. Over low heat, slowly cook down to a thickened consistency, stirring often to avoid scorching, for about 5 minutes.

4. Remove from the heat and cool. Stir in the butter until evenly distributed.

5. Divide the mixture among serving glasses and chill until firm, about 20 minutes.

COCONUT PANNA COTTA

- ¾ cup (175 grams) heavy cream (35% fat)
- ¼ cup (70 grams) granulated sugar
- 2 leaves sheet gelatin, bloomed and squeezed of excess water
- ¾ cup (180 grams) coconut cream or coconut milk

1. Combine cream and sugar. Gently heat to dissolve. Remove from heat and add the bloomed gelatin.

2. Add the coconut cream. Thoroughly mix with an immersion blender.

3. Deposit into the serving glasses on top of the caramelized banana mixture. Chill until set, about 30 minutes.

LIME CREAM

- 2 eggs (about 100 grams)
- ¾ cup (150 grams) granulated sugar
- 6 tablespoons (90 grams) lime juice
- 6 tablespoons (85 grams) unsalted butter

1. In a heavy saucepan, whisk together the eggs and sugar, then add the lime juice.

2. On medium heat, stir constantly until mixture reaches a boil. Remove from heat.

3. Allow the mixture to cool, then emulsify the butter into a cream using a whisk or an immersion blender.

4. Once cooled, but still fluid, divide about half of the mixture among the serving dishes, creating a thin layer on top of the set coconut panna cotta. Refrigerate at least 20 minutes until loosely set.

ORANGE-PAPAYA SALAD

- ¼ cup (60 grams) orange juice
- 2 teaspoons (10 grams) unsalted butter
- pinch cayenne pepper
- 1 cup (120 grams) fresh papaya, peeled, cored, and small-diced

1. In a saucepan over medium heat, gently reduce the orange juice to roughly 1 tablespoon.

2. Remove from the heat and whisk in the butter and a pinch of cayenne pepper to taste.

3. Add the diced papaya and toss to combine. Transfer to a small bowl and allow to cool completely.

PLANTAIN CHIPS

- vegetable or corn oil, as needed
- ½ plantain, peeled, and very thinly sliced
- fine sea salt, as needed
- cayenne pepper, as needed

1. Rinse the plantain slices in cold water and thoroughly pat dry on paper towels.

2. Fill a heavy saucepan with oil (no more than halfway), and heat the oil to 350°F (175°C).

3. In small batches, carefully add the plantain slices to the oil and fry until light golden brown, about 3 to 4 minutes. Remove from the oil, drain on paper towels, and lightly season with salt and cayenne pepper.

TO SERVE

- cilantro leaves, as needed (optional)

1. Remove the previously layered and chilled serving dishes from the refrigerator. Divide the papaya mixture among the individual desserts and finish with a few plantain chips and cilantro leaves, as desired.

TRENDING *for Tomorrow*

COGNITIVE, BEYOND COOKING.
IBM WATSON HELPED INTRODUCE
THE WORLD TO COGNITIVE COMPUTING.
NOW IT'S COOKING UP BREAKTHROUGHS
IN FIELDS LIKE HEALTHCARE AND FINANCE.

IBM COGNITIVE COOKI

IBM.COM

Road

Austin's South by Southwest

(SXSW) is one of the country's largest annual tech and music festivals. It was the perfect place to put Watson's computational creativity on display. But the ethos of SXSW extends far beyond passive consumption. This audience would want to interact with the system.

So Chef Watson arrived on a food truck with chefs James and Michael from the Institute of Culinary Education. A new chat interface allowed consumers to dialog with the system, which recommended ingredients. Visitors could also place votes through social media for Watson dishes, with the ICE chefs creating a unique new version of the winners. In one notable exchange, a French Canadian social media campaign prompted the Watson team to

create a surprising poutine—a popular Québécois comfort food featuring potatoes and cheese. Watson and the chefs in the truck whipped up Peruvian Potato Poutine, which blended flavors from the St. Lawrence Valley and the Andean highlands. Look for the recipe in this chapter!

The 12 dishes in this section represent the spontaneity and creativity of cooking on the road. They also tend to be easier to prepare.

Baltic Apple Pie

With simple shifts in proportion or treatment of the ingredients, the result here could easily go from a sweet pie with savory elements to a savory pie with sweet elements. In this case, the cold-weather cuisines of the Baltics and Scandinavia offer some great inspiration to explore the savory route. I also enjoy when savory pies tend to play with a diner's expectations, as the exterior presentation of a flaky pastry crust doesn't always portray the flavors within.

CHEF WATSON SAYS

SURPRISE

PLEASANTNESS

SYNERGY

Pro Notes and Tips

- This leaner version of a meat pie relies on pork tenderloin, with added smokiness from a brief smoked salt brine. For more richness, add some bacon or fattier cuts of pork.

- The allspice "mayo" is made by setting milk and cream with agar and exploiting its shear-thinning properties. The firm, brittle milk gel softens to a smooth spread simply by processing in a blender.

PORK AND APPLE FILLING

- 1 pound (450 grams) pork tenderloin, trimmed and cut into ¼-inch dice
- 2 cups (450 grams) water
- 2 tablespoons (20 grams) smoked salt
- 1 small Granny Smith apple (120 grams), peeled, cored, and diced
- ¼ cup (50 grams) onion, diced
- 1 clove garlic, minced
  unsalted butter, as needed
  light brown sugar, as needed
  fine sea salt, as needed
- 2 tablespoons (2 grams) parsley, finely chopped
- 2 tablespoons (2 grams) chives, thinly sliced
- 1-1½ pounds (450 to 675 grams) frozen puff pastry sheets
- 1 egg
- 2 teaspoons (10 grams) whole milk
  confectioners sugar, as needed (optional)

1. Brine the pork for 20 minutes, then drain and reserve for assembly. Meanwhile, preheat a small sauté pan and gently sweat the apple, onion, and garlic in a small amount of butter until softened, allowing some of the excess moisture from the apple to evaporate. Season lightly with brown sugar and salt (bear in mind that the pork will be slightly salty from brining).

2. Allow the apple mixture to cool and combine thoroughly with the drained diced pork, parsley, and chives. Reserve for assembly.

3. Temper the frozen puff pastry dough in the refrigerator to allow for cutting. Working quickly, cut 4 to 6 puff pastry discs measuring 6 inches (15 centimeters) in diameter. Cut a second round of 4 to 6 discs measuring 4 inches (10.5 centimeters) in diameter. While assembling the pies, keep the remaining dough under refrigeration to avoid excess softening or loss of shape.

4. Whisk together the egg and milk to create an egg wash. Brush each of the larger discs with a very light coating of egg wash and gently place within a 4-inch (10.5-centimeter) tart ring. Repeat for each pie and arrange the partially assembled pies on a parchment-lined sheet pan.

5. Divide the filling among the rings (about ½ cup into each), gently pressing the filling into the bottom of the rings. Place the smaller discs of puff pastry onto the top of each pie and press the edges together. Fold under to create a crimped edge that extends just above the lip of the tart rings. Lightly brush the surface of each pie with egg wash and, using a small paring knife, make a few small slashes in the surface to allow steam to escape.

6. Bake the pies in an oven preheated to 350°F (175°C) for 10 minutes. Reduce heat to 300°F (150°C) and continue to bake until the exterior is uniformly browned and the pork filling is thoroughly cooked (about 30 minutes). Remove from the heat and dust very lightly with confectioners sugar. Return to the oven briefly for 30 seconds to melt the sugar and cool slightly before unmolding.

BLUEBERRY APRICOT PRESERVE

- ¼ cup (60 grams) blueberries
- 2 tablespoons (20 grams) dried apricot, diced
- ½ cup (125 grams) water
- 1 tablespoon (10 grams) light brown sugar
- 1 teaspoon (3 grams) fresh ginger, peeled, and finely chopped
  fine sea salt, to taste

1. Combine all of the ingredients in a small saucepan and bring to a simmer. Cook on low heat for about 10 minutes, until the fruits have softened.

2. Remove from heat and cool thoroughly. Blend very well, strain through a fine mesh sieve (if desired), and chill.

ALLSPICE "MAYO"

- ½ cup (125 grams) whole milk
- ½ vanilla bean, split and scraped
- ½ teaspoon (2 grams) agar
- ½ cup (100 grams) heavy cream (35% fat)
- 1 egg yolk (about 20 grams)
- 1 teaspoon (10 grams) granulated sugar
  fine sea salt, to taste
- ¼ teaspoon (0.5 gram) ground allspice

1. Combine the milk, vanilla, and agar in a small saucepan. Gently bring to a boil. Reduce heat while maintaining a simmer for 2 minutes. Remove from the heat and whisk in cream, egg yolk, sugar, salt, and allspice. Remove the vanilla pod and allow to cool completely at room temperature and set.

2. Process the gel in a blender until smooth, then chill.

GARLIC CHIPS

- 2-3 garlic cloves, peeled
  whole milk, as needed
  vegetable oil, as needed

1. Slice the garlic very thin and place in a saucepan with milk, just to cover. Bring to a boil, drain the milk, and repeat this blanching process 2 more times. Gently dry the garlic slices on paper towels.

2. Heat the oil to 350°F (175°C) and lightly fry the garlic chips until crisp.

TO SERVE

- Granny Smith apple, as needed
  chives, as needed
  parsley leaves, as needed

1. Slice the peeled and cored apple into a very fine julienne about 1 inch in length. Cut the chives into sticks of similar size.

2. Place a few dollops of the allspice "mayo" and blueberry preserve onto each pie and garnish with the apple julienne, chive sticks, parsley leaves, and garlic chips.

Turkish-Korean Anchovy Caesar Salad

For a Caesar salad created with Watson, regular old croutons just wouldn't do, so I decided to make a rich artichoke purée set with agar that could be diced, coated with bread crumbs, and fried to look just like a typical crouton. Featuring roasted eggplant and sesame oil, the dressing tastes like a spicy, slightly sweet tahini.

Pro Notes and Tips

- Artichoke "croutons" are my over-the-top take on this unique version of Caesar salad. They are crisp with a brown exterior and a creamy, tender filling. For a quicker version, toss sliced artichokes in flour and sauté them in olive oil until crunchy.

- Doenjang is a traditional Korean ingredient. If you're unable to find it, white miso is a common substitute.

ROASTED EGGPLANT PURÉE

- 2 Japanese eggplants (300 grams), cubed, and peeled
- 2 tablespoons (20 grams) doenjang
- 6 branches fresh thyme
- 2 branches basil
- 2 tablespoons (60 grams) soy sauce
- pinch cayenne

1. Combine all ingredients in a bowl and mix well. Place in an 8- by 8-inch (20- by 20-centimeter) pan and cover tightly with foil. Roast in the oven at 350°F (175°C) until very tender, about 45 minutes. Transfer mixture to a food processor and purée until smooth.

DRESSING

- 1 cup (260 grams) roasted eggplant purée
- 2 egg yolks (35 grams)
- ½ teaspoon (1 gram) Korean red pepper flakes
- 2 tablespoons (25 grams) Korean fish sauce
- ⅓ cup (80 grams) grated Parmesan cheese
- 2 teaspoons (5 grams) sesame oil
- 2 tablespoons (24 grams) red wine vinegar
- 2 tablespoons plus 1 teaspoon (35 grams) doenjang

1. Combine all the ingredients in a food processor and purée until smooth.

CROUTONS

- ½ teaspoon (3 grams) sesame oil
- 4 branches fresh thyme
- 1 pound (500 grams) artichoke hearts
- ½ cup (115 grams) orange juice
- pinch cayenne pepper
- 1¼ cups (300 grams) water
- 1 tablespoon (8 grams) agar
- flour, as needed
- egg, as needed
- fresh bread crumbs, as needed

1. Heat the oil in a saucepot, add the thyme, and cook until aromatic. Add the artichokes and sauté until tender. Add the orange juice and cayenne. Cover the pot and simmer until very tender. Purée in a blender until very smooth.

2. In a separate pot, whisk together the water and agar. Bring the mixture to a boil, stirring constantly. Cook at a simmer for 2 minutes. Blend the agar mixture into the artichoke purée. Transfer to a pan to set.

3. Dice the set artichoke purée and pass through the standard breading procedure, rolling the pieces first in flour, then dipping in the beaten egg, and finally coating with bread crumbs. Deep-fry just before serving.

TO SERVE

3 cups (200 grams) napa cabbage, chopped
1 tablespoon (25 grams) orange juice
½ teaspoon (1 gram) Korean red pepper
  salt, as needed
  about 3 cups (250 grams) baby arugula
  shaved Parmesan cheese, as needed

1. Toss the cabbage with the orange juice, red pepper, and salt. Set aside to wilt. Before serving, drain the cabbage, pressing lightly to extract excess liquid.

2. Dress the cabbage with the Caesar dressing. Gently fold in the arugula and top the salad with croutons and Parmesan.

Creole Shrimp-Lamb Dumpling

Having grown up cooking in seafood restaurants on the Florida Panhandle— "just down the road" from New Orleans—I was excited to tackle Creole flavors with Watson. Familiar ingredients like okra and filé powder made me happy, but putting lamb and shrimp together in the same dish was something I had never imagined doing, in any context. The flavors play surprisingly well together, and the result is far greater than the sum of its parts.

Pro Notes and Tips

- The chickpea dumpling wrapper should have a similar texture to a pasta dough. Follow that model for rolling the dough as well. I found pasta rollers gave me the perfect texture and thickness for the dumpling skin.

- Store-bought wonton skins are a fine substitute for the chickpea dough.

1½ cups (200 grams) chickpea flour
3 tablespoons (45 grams) ghee or butter, divided
¾ cup (100 grams) water
4 ounces (115 grams) ground lamb
1 tablespoon (12 grams) kosher salt, divided
1½ teaspoons (6 grams) ground black pepper, divided
¼ cup (35 grams) celery, minced
½ cup (130 grams) canned chopped tomatoes
1 cup (115 grams) chicken stock
½ cup (70 grams) okra, blanched, and small-diced
4 ounces (115 grams) shrimp, chopped
½ teaspoon (2 grams) filé powder
1 tablespoon (6 grams) parsley, chopped
1 tablespoon (15 grams) lemon juice
1 egg, beaten
vegetable oil, as needed

1. Combine the chickpea flour, 2 tablespoons (25 grams) ghee or butter, and water in a food processor and pulse until a dough forms. Tightly wrap the ball of dough and set aside to rest 20 minutes before rolling.

2. In a pan over medium heat, sauté the ground lamb in the remaining ghee or butter. Add ½ tablespoon (6 grams) of salt and ½ teaspoon (2 grams) of black pepper, and cook until well done, stirring regularly. Add the celery and cook for a few minutes, until soft.

3. Add the tomatoes, broth, okra, shrimp, filé powder, and the rest of the salt and black pepper, then simmer over medium heat until reduced. Refrigerate and cool. Mix in the parsley and lemon juice.

4. Roll out dough to ⅛-inch (.3 cm) thick. Cut into 3-inch (7.6 cm) rounds. Drop large spoonfuls of the filling onto each round, and brush with the beaten egg. Fold and press to seal.

5. Fry dumplings at 350°F (175°C) until golden and crisp, or bake on a rack, brushing with oil before placing in the oven.

Vietnamese Apple Kebab

The ingredients in Watson's output initially seemed incompatible (mushroom, strawberry, chicken, pineapple), but all of them share significant levels of the flavor compound g-dodecalactone. The trick here was to create a Vietnamese-inspired dish without the use of familiar flavors like fish sauce, chili peppers, lemongrass, garlic, and cilantro.

CHEF WATSON SAYS

SURPRISE   PLEASANTNESS   SYNERGY

Pro Notes and Tips

• The Vietnamese curry powder is mixed into the meatball mixture, but it is also used as a marinade for the chicken through a pressure-infusion technique, which allows the flavors to penetrate the meat more effectively than through conventional methods. If you don't have a foam canister, the marinating time would increase by roughly 30 to 45 minutes.

PORK MEATBALLS

 1 pound (450 grams) ground pork
 ¼ cup (40 grams) scallion, white portion, finely minced
 ¼ cup (40 grams) Granny Smith apple, brunoise
 1 tablespoon (5 grams) fresh ginger, finely minced
    zest of ½ lime, grated
    zest of ½ lemon, grated
 2 tablespoons (2 grams) fresh mint, finely chopped
 1½ teaspoons (4 grams) Vietnamese curry powder
 ½ teaspoon (2 grams) white pepper
 1 vanilla bean, split and scraped, pod discarded
    fine sea salt, as needed
    lard, as needed

1. Thoroughly mix all ingredients, except for the lard, until combined. Portion and roll the mixture into 24 meatballs, each weighing about ½ ounce (15 grams).

2. Arrange the meatballs in a single layer on a roasting pan lightly greased with lard and place them in an oven preheated to 320°F (160°C) for about 20 minutes (or until thoroughly cooked). Remove from the oven and season as desired.

PRESSURE-INFUSED CURRY CHICKEN

 ½ cup (160 grams) water
 3 tablespoons (40 grams) vegetable oil
 1 tablespoon (15 grams) lime juice
 1 tablespoon (15 grams) lemon juice
 2 tablespoons (15 grams) Vietnamese curry powder
 12 ounces (340 grams) chicken breast, trimmed and cut into 24 bite-sized pieces
    fine sea salt, as needed

1. Whisk together the water, oil, lime juice, lemon juice, and curry powder.

2. Place the chicken breast pieces and the curry mixture into a half-liter foam canister, seal, and dispense two N_2O chargers. Gently shake to distribute and allow to stand for 5 minutes. Slowly release the pressure, empty the contents into a shallow pan, and chill.

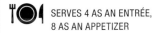 SERVES 4 AS AN ENTRÉE, 8 AS AN APPETIZER

 1 HOUR, PLUS MARINATING AND BAKING

 MICHAEL LAISKONIS

3. Transfer the chicken and remaining marinade into a shallow saucepan over low heat, stirring, until chicken is thoroughly cooked. Season to taste and allow the chicken to cool in the marinade.

PINEAPPLE BROTH
1 cup (225 grams) pineapple juice
1 vanilla bean, split and scraped
1 tablespoon (5 grams) ginger, finely minced
1 tablespoon (15 grams) lime juice
1 teaspoon (5 grams) lemon juice
  zest of ½ lime, grated
  zest of ½ lemon, grated
  salt, as needed
  white pepper, as needed
¼ teaspoon (1 gram) xanthan gum (optional)

1. Combine the pineapple juice, vanilla, ginger, lime juice, lemon juice, and zests. Gently heat to 140°F (60°C). Cover and allow to infuse for 1 hour.

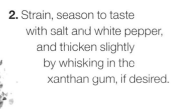

2. Strain, season to taste with salt and white pepper, and thicken slightly by whisking in the xanthan gum, if desired.

PICKLED CARROT AND SHIITAKE MUSHROOM
2 medium shiitake mushrooms (about 40 grams), thinly sliced
1 tablespoon (10 grams) vegetable oil
  white pepper, as needed
  fine sea salt, as needed
1 small carrot (about 80 grams), peeled, and julienned
1 tablespoon (5 grams) ginger, finely minced
1 tablespoon (15 grams) lime juice
1 tablespoon (15 grams) lemon juice

1. In a medium-size sauté pan, gently cook the mushrooms in the vegetable oil just until softened and season to taste.

2. Add the carrot, ginger, lime juice, and lemon juice. Over low heat, slowly reduce until liquid has absorbed. Remove from heat.

3. Allow to cool. Adjust seasoning and acidity as desired.

TO SERVE
¼ cup (40 grams) Granny Smith apple, julienned
¼ cup (45 grams) cucumber, finely diced
¼ cup (45 grams) strawberry, finely diced
2 scallions, green portion, thinly sliced and held in ice water
2 sprigs of fresh mint leaves, torn
12 pieces chives, sliced into ⅓-inch (1-centimeter) lengths
  zest of ½ lime, grated
  Maldon salt, as needed
  white pepper, as needed

1. To serve as an entrée, arrange 6 of the warmed pork meatballs and 4 pieces of the chicken into each bowl. Top with a small amount of the apple, cucumber, and strawberry followed by the pickled carrot and shiitake mixture. As an appetizer, use half the amount.

2. Pour a small amount of the warmed pineapple broth into the dish and finish with the scallions, mint, chives, and lime zest. Season with Maldon salt and an additional grind of white pepper.

Austrian Chocolate Burrito

With this dish, I challenged myself (and Watson) by calling out two elements not associated with a burrito: Austrian cuisine and chocolate. And without much technical fanfare, I gave the conventional burrito surprising character and complexity. Using edamame as the bean, alongside apricot and orange, added a freshness that balanced the ground beef and undertones of chocolate and spice.

CHEF WATSON SAYS

SURPRISE

PLEASANTNESS

SYNERGY

Pro Notes and Tips

- Sometimes Watson surprises us by what *isn't* among the output ingredients. In this case it was heat, in the form of either dried or fresh chili peppers. If you need a kick, add a touch of fresh sliced jalapeño or smoky chipotle pepper.

- This recipe swaps the cheese curds suggested by the original output with a more authentic queso fresco or Cotija cheese.

- The larger burritos could be cut into smaller pieces and served as an appetizer.

BEEF FILLING

- 1 pound (450 grams) lean ground beef, browned and drained of excess fat
- zest of 1 orange, grated
- pinch ground cinnamon
- 1 ounce (30 grams) dark chocolate (70% cocoa solids or higher), very finely chopped
- fine sea salt, as needed

1. While the browned ground beef is still warm, stir in the orange zest, cinnamon, and chocolate. Season with salt to taste and reserve for assembly.

COCOA-APRICOT PURÉE

- ½ cup (120 grams) apricot purée
- ½ vanilla bean, split and scraped
- ½ ounce (15 grams) dark chocolate (70% cocoa solids or higher), very finely chopped

1. Combine the apricot purée and vanilla in a saucepan. Slowly reduce over medium heat to roughly ¼ cup. Remove from heat and stir in the chocolate. Cool and reserve for assembly.

MASHED EDAMAME

- 1½ cups (160 grams) edamame, shelled
- water, as needed
- salt, as needed

1. Blanch the edamame in boiling salted water for about 1 minute. Drain and shock in ice water.

2. Transfer the edamame to a food processor and pulse to achieve a rough textured paste. Season with salt and reserve for assembly.

TO SERVE

- 6 flour tortillas, 10-inch (25-centimeter) diameter
- vegetable shortening, melted, as needed (optional)
- 1 cup (85 grams) grated Edam cheese
- ½ cup (100 grams) crumbled queso fresco or Cotija cheese
- dark chocolate, as needed

1. Gently warm each tortilla in a hot, dry pan or on a griddle. Arrange the tortilla on a flat work surface and very lightly brush the top half with shortening (this will help to bind the wrap and hold it together).

2. In the center of the tortilla, arrange the ground beef mixture, mashed edamame, and Edam cheese. Top with some of the apricot purée.

3. Tightly roll from the bottom up, and top with queso fresco and grated chocolate.

 SERVES 6   🕐 45 MINUTES    MICHAEL LAISKONIS

Caribbean Snapper Fish and Chips

This output allowed me to make a proper fish and chips, just as they would in the Caribbean (I imagine), with spicy, cornmeal-crusted snapper and plantain chips. And that is how I cooked it the first time. While delicious, it was too simple and expected. So I reimagined what a fish and chips could be: snapper ceviche with tropical-flavored cornmeal fritters and spicy fennel slaw. The result was a hit at SXSW—unexpected with lots of big, bold flavors.

CHEF WATSON SAYS

SURPRISE   PLEASANTNESS   SYNERGY

Pro Notes and Tips

- There are 3 rules for making ceviche: 1. Buy the freshest fish possible. 2. Buy the freshest fish possible. 3. Buy the freshest fish possible. Once you've done that, the rest is simple.

- While the fish needs an hour or so to cure in the lime juice, be careful not to leave it too long. After 5 hours or so, the fish can become tough or a bit dry.

½ cup (115 grams) coconut cream
3 fluid ounces (85 grams) lime juice
1 serrano pepper, minced
2 heads fennel
  salt and ground black pepper, as needed
12 ounces (350 grams) boneless, skinless snapper filet
1 teaspoon (3 grams) ground coriander seeds
½ teaspoon (2 grams) smoked serrano powder, divided
1 cup (140 grams) yellow cornmeal
8 fluid ounces (225 grams) coconut milk
1 egg, separated
2 cups (120 grams) plantain chips
  Tajin Chili Lime seasoning, as needed
  vegetable oil, as needed

1. To make the slaw, whisk together the coconut cream and 2 tablespoons (30 grams) of the lime juice. Add ½ of the serrano pepper to the coconut mixture.

2. Shave on a mandoline or thinly slice the fennel. Reserve the ends and odd pieces of fennel to mince for the fritter. Toss the shaved fennel with the coconut mixture and combine well to coat. Season to taste with salt and ground black pepper.

3. Cut the fish into thin slices and lay in a shallow baking dish. Season each piece with the coriander and smoked serrano. Pour over 2 fluid ounces (55 grams) of the lime juice, gently mix, and refrigerate at least 1 hour before serving.

4. For the fritters, mix the cornmeal, coconut milk, ½ cup (70 grams) minced fennel, the remaining serrano, and the egg yolk. Stir until the batter is smooth.

5. In a separate bowl, whip the egg white to soft peaks and fold into the batter.

6. Heat 1 inch of oil in a wide, shallow pan. Drop spoonfuls of the batter into the hot oil. Cook until crisp.

7. To serve, place a fritter in the center of each plate. Top with fennel slaw and place a spoonful of ceviche next to the fennel. Garnish with plantain chips seasoned with the Tajin.

Indonesian Rice Chili Con Carne

Vanilla and tomatoes make an outstanding flavor combination. What is missing in this dish is the spice. Cubeb—which I had never heard of until it came up in this output—is a very aromatic cousin of the peppercorn, but brings no heat to the dish. If you do like heat, try adding some minced jalapeño to the chili base.

CHEF WATSON SAYS

SURPRISE   PLEASANTNESS   **SYNERGY**

Pro Notes and Tips

• When buying fresh lemongrass, look for whole stalks that are pale at the base, possibly with a hint of pink or red and light green at the top. (The stalks should be firm but should not look dry or brown at the edges).

ROASTED PORK BELLY

- 1 pound (500 grams) pork belly, cut into ½-inch cubes
- 2 teaspoons (9 grams) kosher salt
- 2 teaspoons (8 grams) cubeb pepper
- ¾ cup (170 grams) lager-style beer

1. Combine the pork with the salt and cubeb. Toss well to coat.

2. Transfer the pork to a large sauté or small roasting pan. Roast in a convection oven at 500°F (260°C) until well browned. Drain the fat from the roasting pan and deglaze with the beer.

CHILI BASE

- 4 tablespoons (60 grams) butter
- ¼ cup (30 grams) scallions, thinly sliced
- ¼ cup (45 grams) celery, thinly sliced
- 1 piece lemongrass
- 1½ teaspoons (6 grams) ground black pepper
  pinch ground cloves
- 1 teaspoon (4 grams) cubeb pepper
- 2 cups (500 grams) chicken stock
- 3½ cups (790 grams) canned tomatoes
- ½ vanilla bean, split
- 1 pound (500 grams) skirt steak
  kosher salt, as needed

1. While the pork is cooking, begin the chili base. Melt the butter in a saucepot. Add the scallions and celery, and sauté until tender.

2. Cut a 2-inch piece of lemongrass from the base and smash with the back of a knife. (Reserve remaining lemongrass for the skirt steak.) In a sauce pot, add the chicken stock plus black pepper, cubeb, and clove. Bring the mixture to a boil and reduce by half. Add the tomato and vanilla. Season to taste with salt and reduce the heat to simmer. Add the pork and beer, then cover the pot and transfer to the oven, and cook for 2 hours at 325°F (160°C).

SKIRT STEAK

- 1 pound (500 grams) skirt steak
- 1 teaspoon (4 grams) kosher salt
- 2 tablespoons (20 grams) lemongrass, minced
- 1 teaspoon (4 grams) ground black pepper

1. Trim the skirt steak and season with salt. Combine the lemongrass and black pepper. Use the mixture to marinate the steak, 2 hours to overnight.

2. Quickly char the steak on the grill. (Do not worry if the meat is still very rare).

3. Thinly slice the steak and cut into ½-inch lengths. Fold into the chili base.

PICKLED VEGETABLES

- 1 cup (225 grams) rice vinegar
- 1 teaspoon (4 grams) kosher salt
- 1 tablespoon (9 grams) sugar
- 4 tablespoons (30 grams) lemongrass, sliced
- 1 teaspoon (2 grams) black peppercorns
- 1 tablespoon (6 grams) dill
- 1 cup (160 grams) green beans, blanched and shocked
- ¼ cup (30 grams) scallions, julienned

1. Combine the vinegar, salt, sugar, lemongrass, and peppercorns in a medium saucepot and bring to a boil. Remove from the heat and cool completely.

2. Add the dill, green beans, and scallions. Let the vegetables pickle overnight.

TO SERVE

- 1 cup (225 grams) green peas, blanched and shocked
- 2 cups (400 grams) cooked rice
- ¼ cup (20 grams) micro celery

1. Mix the warm rice and peas. Place a small spoonful of the mixture in each bowl.

2. Top with the tomato-braised pork belly and beef chili. Garnish with pickled vegetables and micro celery.

Moroccan Almond Curry

Interestingly, Watson went an old-fashioned route here, building a curry-like flavor profile using typical aromatic spices. The one outlier is the romaine lettuce. Though it's not uncommon to present lettuce in cooked form, here I used it (and the peas, to some extent) as a fresh and crisp contrast to the heavier lamb flavors.

Pro Notes and Tips

- This dish could easily be cooked in one go, with the components prepared and plated as the lamb finishes its braising. However, it is convenient to break up parts of the process in advance; I also find that moist, ultra-tender meat relies in part on slowly cooling while still submerged in the cooking liquid.

- In place of the pea purée, fresh or frozen peas could easily be added to the rice during the final moments of cooking.

CURRY-BRAISED LAMB

- ½ teaspoon (0.5 gram) ground cardamom
- ½ teaspoon (0.5 gram) ground cumin
- 1 teaspoon (0.5 gram) ground turmeric
- 2 teaspoons (1 gram) ground Spanish paprika
- 4 lamb shanks
  salt, as needed
  vegetable oil, as needed
- 1 rib celery (about 40 grams), chopped
- 2 plum tomatoes (about 225 grams), coarsely chopped
- 1 cup (225 grams) orange juice
  zest of 1 orange
  water, as needed

1. Over low heat, gently toast the spices in a dry sauté pan until aromatic. Remove from the heat and reserve.

2. Season the lamb shanks with salt and place in a hot sauté pan with a small amount of vegetable oil. Thoroughly brown on all sides. Remove the shanks from the pan and discard oil.

3. Using the same pan, sauté the celery and the chopped tomato. Deglaze the pan with the orange juice and zest. Add the reserved spices and remove from heat.

4. Combine the lamb shanks, vegetables, and deglazing mixture in a shallow baking dish or ovenproof pan with a tight-fitting lid. Ensure that the shanks are mostly submerged, adding additional water as necessary.

5. On the stove top, gently bring the pan to a simmer. Remove from heat, place the lid onto the pan (or wrap tightly with aluminum foil), and place in an oven preheated to 275°F (135°C) and slowly braise for 4 to 5 hours.

6. Remove the pan from the oven and allow the lamb shanks to cool to room temperature in the braising liquid.

7. When cool, defat and strain the braising liquid. Place in a small saucepan and bring to a simmer. Gently reduce the cooking liquid by roughly half. Reserve.

PEA PURÉE

1½ cups frozen peas, thawed
    water, as needed
    fine sea salt, as needed

1. Blanch the peas in boiling salted water for 1 to 2 minutes. Drain and shock in ice water to halt the cooking process.

2. Place the peas in a high-power blender and begin to process, adding just enough water (about ¼ cup or 50 grams) to produce a thick, smooth purée. Season with salt and reserve.

BASMATI RICE

2¾ cups (500 grams) water
  1 teaspoon (5 grams) fine sea salt
1½ cups (250 grams) basmati rice

1. Place the water and salt in a medium-size saucepan with a tight-fitting lid. Bring to a boil.

2. Stir in the rice, reduce heat to low, and cover. Cook for 12 to 15 minutes and remove from the heat. Allow to stand covered for 5 minutes.

3. Gently fluff the rice with a fork before serving.

TO SERVE

¼ cup (45 grams) slivered almonds, lightly toasted and chopped
    pea shoots, as needed
    celery leaves, as needed
    romaine lettuce (inner leaves of the heart), as needed, sliced into bite-sized pieces
    fine sea salt, as needed
    vegetable oil, as needed
    cilantro leaves, as needed

1. Place the lamb shanks and reduced cooking liquid in a shallow covered pan and warm in a preheated 350°F (175°C) oven for 20 to 30 minutes.

2. Meanwhile, toss the pea shoots, celery leaves, and romaine pieces in a spoonful of oil and season with salt.

3. Plate the warmed lamb shank, along with a portion of the rice and a spoonful of the pea purée. Season the cooking liquid with salt and spoon over the lamb or serve on the side. Finish each plate with a sprinkle of the almonds and the dressed pea shoots, celery, and romaine leaves, followed by cilantro.

#IBMFoodTruck
#Curry

Moroccan Almond Curry

Portuguese Lobster Roll

This is probably one of the most complex dishes I created with Watson. It was meant to be a showstopper for our first public appearances at the Pulse Conference and at SXSW. While the presentation may be over-the-top, don't be afraid to experiment with this dish's flavors—olive, saffron, basil, lobster, and balsamic—in a more rustic preparation and presentation.

CHEF WATSON SAYS

SURPRISE   PLEASANTNESS   SYNERGY

Pro Notes and Tips

- Transglutaminase, sold under the name Activa, is also known as "meat glue." It is a natural enzyme that causes proteins to bond to one another. It is by no means necessary for this recipe, but it allows for a dramatic presentation with the trio of sauces.

ROMESCO RED PEPPER COULIS

- 2 tablespoons (30 grams) olive oil
- ½ cup (30 grams) bread, cubed
- 2 red bell peppers, roasted, peeled, and seeded
- 1½ cups (250 grams) Roma tomatoes, chopped
  pinch red pepper flakes

1. Heat the olive oil in a saucepot. Add the bread and cook until well toasted. Add the roasted peppers, tomato, and red pepper flakes. Cover and cook until very tender. Purée in a blender until smooth.

SAFFRON FLUID GEL

- 2 tablespoons (30 grams) olive oil
- 1 teaspoon (2 grams) coriander seeds
- 1½ cups (210 grams) carrots, thinly sliced
- 1 bay leaf
  pinch saffron
- 2 cups (500 grams) water
  1% agar by weight (0.01 x weight of purée, approximately 350 grams)
  0.15% xanthan gum (0.0015 x weight of purée, approximately 350 grams)
  lemon juice, as needed
  kosher salt, as needed

1. Heat the olive oil in a saucepot. Add the coriander and cook until toasted. Add the carrots, bay leaf, and saffron. Sauté 3 to 5 minutes, without browning.

2. Add water and cover the pot. Simmer until completely tender. Strain the liquid and discard the vegetables.

3. Measure the agar and xanthan by weight, whisk into the liquid, and return to a clean pan. Whisk until the mixture returns to a boil, and cook 1 minute more. Pour into a pan to set.

4. When set, break up the gel, place in a blender, and add water until a smooth, but very thick, purée forms. Season to taste with lemon juice and salt.

BASIL MAYO

- ½ cup (150 grams) packed basil, blanched, shocked, and squeezed dry
- 2½ tablespoons (150 grams) water
- 0.67 gram xanthan gum
- 1 cup (200 grams) mayonnaise
- kosher salt, as needed

1. Combine the basil and water in a blender, and purée until smooth. With the blender running, add the xanthan gum and process for 5 seconds. Whisk the basil purée into the mayo and season to taste.

LOBSTER

- 1½ pounds (675 grams) lobster meat
- 0.3 ounces (10 grams) Activa RM

1. Coarsely chop the lobster meat, sprinkle with the Activa, and mix well. Transfer the meat to a vacuum bag and seal. Press the meat into an even form and leave overnight to set. Then cook sous vide for 15 minutes at 125°F (52°C).

CRISPY PULLED PORK

- 2 tablespoons (18 grams) Worcestershire sauce
- ¼ cup (45 grams) tomato paste
- 2 tablespoons (15 grams) balsamic vinegar
- 2.2 pounds (1,000 grams) pork ribs
- vegetable oil, as needed

1. Whisk the Worcestershire, tomato paste, and balsamic vinegar together to form a smooth paste. Season the pork with salt and pepper, then coat generously with the tomato mixture. Seal the pork ribs in a vacuum bag and cook sous vide at 162°F (72°C) for 24 hours. Cool the meat slightly and shred.

2. In preparation for serving, heat a pot of oil to 400°F (205°C) and fry the shredded meat until crisp.

TO SERVE

- mini hot dog buns
- 8 pieces of lettuce
- 2 tablespoons (20 grams) green olives, minced
- micro basil, as needed

1. Slice the lobster into "planks" the size of the buns.

2. Cut the hot dog buns in half and spread some of the basil mayo on the cut sides. Lay a leaf of lettuce on each bun and top with the lobster.

3. Finish the lobster with a squeeze of lemon juice, then dot with red pepper, saffron, and basil sauces. Sprinkle the olives over the lobster, and pile the crisp pork and micro basil on top.

Peruvian Potato Poutine

A dish I was completely unprepared to create at SXSW was poutine—a French Canadian specialty. First, Florian Pinel had to teach Watson more about this unexpected crowd favorite, since the system only contained one poutine recipe at the time. Once Watson received a poutine crash course, we were up and running, blending 5 gallons of tomato sauce on the bumper of the food truck (yes, we have the photos).

Pro Notes and Tips

- To take your poutine to the next level, try making your own french fries. Cut the potatoes into batons and rinse them well. Fry them once in low-temperature oil (300°F/150°C), then cool completely before frying again at a higher temperature (375°F/190°C).

BACON-TOMATO GRAVY

- ½ pound (250 grams) sliced bacon
- 2 cups (500 grams) onion, diced
- 1 teaspoon (1 gram) fresh thyme leaves
- 1 teaspoon (3 grams) ground cumin
- ¼ teaspoon (0.5 gram) cayenne
  pinch ground cloves
- ½ cup (65 grams) whole wheat flour
- 2 cups (500 grams) chicken stock
- 3½ cups (790 grams) canned crushed tomatoes
  salt and pepper, as needed

1. Cook the bacon until crisp and reserve the fat. Drain on paper towels. When cooled, chop into bite-size pieces and reserve.

2. Strain the bacon fat into a clean sauté pan set over medium heat. Add the onion and cook until caramelized, about 25 minutes. Add the thyme, cumin, cayenne, and cloves. Cook until aromatic, about 1 minute.

3. Add the flour and cook, stirring constantly to a roux. Add the stock and mix until smooth. Simmer until fully thickened. Add the tomatoes and cook 15 minutes more. Transfer the mixture to a blender and process until smooth. Season to taste with salt and pepper.

ROASTED CAULIFLOWER

- 1 head cauliflower
- 1 teaspoon (3 grams) kosher salt
- 1 teaspoon (3 grams) ground cumin
- 1 teaspoon (1 gram) fresh thyme leaves
  Shortening (or olive oil), as needed

1. Trim the cauliflower into bite-sized florets, toss with the salt, cumin, and thyme. Spread the seasoned vegetables out on a sheet pan brushed with shortening. Roast in an oven set to 450°F (230°C) until browned on the edges (about 12 minutes).

TO SERVE

3   cups (750 grams) cooked
    french fries

1   cup (90 grams) queso blanco, crumbled

1. Divide the cooked fries equally among 4 plates. Top the fries with the roasted cauliflower and bacon. Spoon a generous amount of the tomato gravy over the top and finish with queso fresco.

Bengali Butternut BBQ Sauce

The output here had all of the required elements for a typical barbecue sauce—sweet, sour, spice, and heat—but the challenge was in adapting it to the all-American notion of barbecue. When cooked, the squash revealed its subtle sweetness and became the base for all the other flavors. The white wine and butter stood out as the surprising ingredients, but once the sauce began to take shape I noticed that the wine provided a tart, fruity balance, while the butter added depth.

CHEF WATSON SAYS

SURPRISE

PLEASANTNESS

SYNERGY

Pro Notes and Tips

• This sauce is a great example of how several ingredients combine to create a whole that's greater than the sum of its parts. Fresh turmeric root and a tiny Thai chili pepper add to the vibrant flavor, but substituting roughly ¼ teaspoon of dry turmeric powder and ¼ teaspoon chili flakes will work just fine.

 MAKES ABOUT 2½ CUPS (20 FLUID OUNCES)

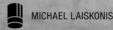 45 MINUTES

MICHAEL LAISKONIS

2 cups (300 grams) butternut squash, diced
3 tablespoons (45 grams) butter, unsalted
scant ½ cup (100 grams) rice vinegar
1 teaspoon (5 grams) tamarind concentrate
3 tablespoons (40 grams) water
⅔ cup (200 grams) white wine
2 teaspoons (10 grams) chili paste (such as Sriracha)
1 teaspoon (5 grams) soy sauce
¼ cup (50 grams) pitted dates, chopped
1 fresh Thai chili, stemmed and halved
1 teaspoon (3 grams) mustard seeds
1 teaspoon (3 grams) fresh turmeric, thinly sliced
¼ teaspoon (0.5 gram) ground cardamom
¼ cup (5 grams) fresh cilantro leaves

1 teaspoon (5 grams) salt, as needed
2 teaspoons (10 grams) Meyer lemon juice
(and zest of half a Meyer lemon, optional)
1 teaspoon (6 grams) molasses

1. Preheat a medium-size saucepan over low heat and gently sweat the squash in the butter until softened (5 to 10 minutes).

2. Add the vinegar, tamarind, water, wine, chili paste, and soy sauce. Increase the heat and bring to a boil, then reduce the heat to low. Add the dates, chili, mustard seeds, turmeric, and cardamom. Continue to simmer at 185°F (85°C) for about 20 minutes.

3. Remove sauce from heat. Add the coriander leaves and cool slightly. In a blender, process the mixture to a very smooth consistency.

4. Season the mixture with salt, lemon juice, and molasses to taste. Chill.

Belgian Bacon Pudding

Bacon-flavored desserts are no longer uncommon, so we chose the popular ingredient as a launching point, in search of more unusual flavor pairings. Watson suprised us with mushroom, cumin, and caraway. The intent here was to present a decidedly sweet flavor, accented with smoky umami notes from the bacon and mushroom and balanced by the acidity of buttermilk. The dried fruits and olive oil-walnut financier provide textural contrast.

CHEF WATSON SAYS

SURPRISE   PLEASANTNESS   SYNERGY

Pro Notes and Tips

- Although there are no actual pieces of bacon in this dish, its smoky flavor is thoroughly extracted through an infusion process known as fat washing, a technique used by many chefs and mixologists.

- If ground walnut meal is unavailable, make your own by grinding ½ cup walnut pieces in a food processor with a portion of the confectioners sugar called for in the recipe.

BACON-PORCINI PUDDING

1	cup (225 grams) whole milk	
2	cups (400 grams) heavy cream	
5	ounces (150 grams) double-smoked bacon, rendered, meat and fat reserved	
2	teaspoons (5 grams) dried porcini mushroom powder	
¼	teaspoon (1 gram) coarsely ground black pepper	
¾	cup (150 grams) granulated sugar	
2	egg yolks (about 40 grams)	
3	leaves sheet gelatin, bloomed in cold water	
¾	cup (85 grams) buttermilk	

1. Combine the milk and cream in a small saucepan and gently heat to about 150°F (65°C). Add the warm rendered bacon meat and fat, and infuse for at least 4 to 6 hours, while chilling.

2. After infusing, strain the cream mixture and discard the bacon and congealed fat solids. Add the mushroom powder and black pepper. Bring to a boil. Meanwhile, whisk together the sugar and egg yolks.

3. Slowly temper the hot cream into the yolk mixture and return to low heat, cooking just to 185°F (85°C). Remove from heat and add the gelatin.

4. Temper the mixture into the buttermilk and blend well with an immersion blender.

5. Divide among 6 glasses or serving dishes, and chill for at least 2 hours, or until set.

WALNUT FINANCIER

7	tablespoons (105 grams) unsalted butter	
½	cup (75 grams) finely ground walnut meal	
½	cup (80 grams) all purpose flour	
	pinch fine sea salt	
½	teaspoon (1.5 grams) baking powder	
1¼	cup (140 grams) confectioners sugar	
4	egg whites (about 120 grams)	
2	tablespoons (20 grams) extra-virgin olive oil	

1. Place the butter in a small saucepan and gently cook over low heat to a light-brown color. Remove from heat and reserve warm.

2. Combine the walnut meal, flour, salt, baking powder, and confectioners sugar in a mixing bowl.

3. In another large mixing bowl, manually whip the egg whites just until frothy. Whisk in the walnut mixture.

4. Slowly whisk in the warm butter, followed by the olive oil, ensuring complete emulsification. Chill for 1 hour.

5. Pipe the mixture into silicone baking molds. Bake at 300°F (150°C) until lightly browned and cooked through, 15 to 20 minutes. Cool and break cakes into small pieces.

SPICED DRIED FRUIT COMPOTE

    juice and zest of 1 orange (about 50 grams)
1 tablespoon (15 grams) honey
    pinch ground cumin
    pinch ground caraway
½ cup (75 grams) golden raisins
½ cup (80 grams) dried figs, stemmed, and coarsely chopped
¼ cup (30 grams) walnuts, coarsely chopped

1. Combine the orange juice and zest, honey, and spices. Pour the orange-honey mixture over the raisins, chopped figs, and walnuts, and macerate several hours, chilled.

TO SERVE

    Maldon salt, as needed
    confectioners sugar, as needed

1. Divide the dried fruit mixture among each set pudding and top with torn financier pieces. Garnish with a few grains of Maldon salt and a dusting of confectioners sugar.

3 A Tasting Menu

In Austin

The night before hundreds of tech and music aficionados were introduced to the Chef Watson food truck at South by Southwest in Austin, Chefs Michael and James from the Institute of Culinary Education were cooking up a delectable feast for 20 technology luminaries.

The menu consisted of seven incredible recipes that told the Chef Watson story. Each dish received a rating for its level of surprise, the number of its ingredients that shared chemical properties (synergy), and pleasantness. This was based on "hedonic psychophysics," a field based on data concerning what people find pleasant (or otherwise).

As usual, the ingredients Watson suggested posed some challenges. The Czech Pork Belly Moussaka, for example, included no eggplant. (The system must have read somewhere that in certain regions of the world moussaka is made with potatoes instead.)

Chef Watson also proposed a cocktail for the feast in Austin: Ivorian Bourbon Punch. The flavors of Tennessee bourbon, fresh fruit and spices from the Ivory Coast combine beautifully. Recommendation: Don't consume too many while preparing the Italian Roast Duck recipes. Both are a little tricky and require a clear mind.

GINGER, CHERRY, FENNEL, CINNAMON, CELERY, OIL, WHITE VINEGAR, WINE,

Italian Roast Duck

"The surprise factor here was not with any one particular ingredient, but rather with looking at the combination of ingredients as a whole. There were many logical pairings with duck—cherry, olive, and cinnamon—but I wouldn't normally think of including all those elements within a single dish."

—MICHAEL LAISKONIS

82

BLACK OLIVE, MUSHROOM, OLIVE, SALT, SAGE, BASIL, DUCK, LARD, TOMATO

" Salt and sweet is a well loved pairing, but the combination of olive and cherry is so unexpected that it truly stands out among the many incredible flavors of this dish. "

—JAMES BRISCIONE

James' Italian Roast Duck

Salt and sweet is a well loved pairing, but the combination of olive and cherry is so unexpected that it truly stands out among the many incredible flavors of this dish.

CHEF WATSON SAYS

SURPRISE   PLEASANTNESS   SYNERGY

Pro Notes and Tips

- If you do not have the equipment to make the vacuum-poached apples in this recipe, do not skip them! The flavor of apples gently cooked in olive oil and scented with sage is incredible. Place the apple wedges, olive oil, and sage in a pan covered with aluminum foil, then cook them in the oven at 250°F (120°C) until just tender, about 20 minutes.

PICKLED MUSHROOMS
2.2 pounds (1,000 grams) king oyster mushrooms
3 cups (700 grams) white vinegar
kosher salt, to taste
½ cup (150 grams) celery, thinly sliced
1 tablespoon (8 grams) fennel seeds
4 branches fresh sage
1 cup (225 grams) extra virgin olive oil

1. Slice the mushrooms lengthwise ½-inch thick (1¼ cm) and score in a crosshatch pattern. Place the mushrooms in a large bowl and toss with a generous amount of salt (use enough to completely coat). Lay the salted mushrooms on a tray and leave for 2 hours to drain. Rinse the mushrooms and press dry with towels.

2. Combine the vinegar, celery, fennel seeds, and sage in a small saucepot. Bring to a boil, add the mushrooms, and simmer 3 minutes. Remove the mushrooms and lay out on towels to drain. Leave the mushrooms to dry overnight. Place the dried mushrooms in a jar or vacuum bag, cover with olive oil, and seal.

VACUUM-POACHED APPLE
4 Golden Delicious apples, peeled, cored, and cut into wedges
2 tablespoons (28 grams) olive oil
1 sprig fresh sage
pinch salt

1. Combine all of the ingredients in a vacuum bag and cook sous vide at (185°F) 85°C for 25 minutes. Reserve.

SHAVED-FENNEL SALAD
1 tablespoon (8 grams) fresh ginger, finely grated
1 tablespoon (8 grams) white vinegar
pinch fennel seeds, ground
2 tablespoons (25 grams) extra-virgin olive oil
kosher salt, to taste
ground black pepper, to taste
2 fennel bulbs

1. Combine the ginger, vinegar, and fennel seeds in a small bowl. Set aside to marinate, 5 minutes. Whisk in the olive oil and season to taste with salt and pepper.

2. Thinly slice the fennel on a mandoline. Place in a bowl and toss with the dressing, as needed.

DUCK SAUSAGE
- 1 pound, 10 ounces (750 grams) boneless duck meat
- 1 tablespoon (14 grams) kosher salt
- 1 teaspoon (5 grams) sel rose (curing salt)
- 1 tablespoon (3 grams) rubbed sage
- 1 tablespoon plus 1 teaspoon (12 grams) black pepper, coarsely ground
- 1 tablespoon (8 grams) fennel seeds
- ¾ teaspoon (2 grams) cinnamon, ground
- 2 teaspoons (5 grams) ginger, ground
- ½ teaspoon (2 grams) cayenne
- 9 ounces (250 grams) pork fat, chilled
- ½ cup (50 grams) dried cherries
- ¼ cup plus 1 tablespoon (75 grams) ice water
  sausage casings, as needed

1. Combine the duck meat, salts, sage, pepper, fennel, cinnamon, ginger, and cayenne in a bowl and mix well. Transfer the mixture to a baking pan and place in the freezer until partially frozen.

2. Combine the duck mixture with the pork fat and dried cherries, and pass through a meat grinder. Place the ground meat and ice water in a bowl and mix. Stuff the mixture into casings and rest 4 hours to overnight.

3. Place the cased sausage in a large, wide pot and cover with water by 2 inches (5 cm). Gently bring the pot to a light simmer and turn off the heat. Leave the sausage in the water to rest for 30 minutes.

4. Cut the sausage into pieces and brown in a sauté pan. Transfer the pieces to the tomato sauce (recipe follows) and simmer for 15 minutes before serving.

PORCINI-RED WINE TOMATO SAUCE
- olive oil, as needed
- 1 cup (250 grams) fennel, minced
- ½ cup (100 grams) celery, minced
- ¼ cup (50 grams) olives, minced
- 1 cup (225 grams) red wine
- ½ cup (15 grams) dried porcini mushrooms
- 6 sprigs sage
- 6 sprigs basil
- 1 teaspoon (3 grams) black pepper
- 1½ teaspoons (5 grams) fennel seeds
- 4 cups (1,000 grams) canned San Marzano tomatoes, chopped
  kosher salt, to taste

1. Heat the olive oil in a large saucepot. Add the fennel and celery, and sweat until tender. Stir in the olives and deglaze with red wine.

2. Tie the porcini, sage, basil, pepper, and fennel in cheesecloth, and add to the pot. When the wine is reduced by half, add the tomatoes and bring the mixture to a simmer. Cool, covered 1 hour over low heat. Discard the sachet and season to taste with salt.

BLACK OLIVE AND DRIED CHERRY COULIS
- ½ cup (100 grams) dried cherries
- 1 cup (225 grams) red wine
- 2 sprigs sage
- 1 cup (200 grams) pitted Niçoise olives with brine

1. Combine the cherries, wine, and sage in a saucepot. Bring the mixture to a simmer and set aside for 5 minutes as the cherries plump.

2. Discard the sage and drain any remaining wine. Combine the cherries and olives in a blender, and process until smooth.

TO SERVE
  fried sage leaves, as needed

1. Make a line of the olive-cherry coulis across the bottom of the plate. Place pickled mushrooms on both ends of the line. Arrange pieces of the sausage next to the coulis and drop in a few pieces of the apple. Top with some of the tomato sauce. Garnish with shaved fennel and fried sage leaves.

Michael's Italian Roast Duck

The surprise factor here was not with any one particular ingredient, but rather with looking at the combination of ingredients as a whole. There were many logical pairings with duck—cherry, olive, and cinnamon—but I wouldn't normally think of including all those elements within a single dish. I looked to the Alto Adige region of Italy to pick up on the bordering German and Austrian influences, in an effort to lighten the conventional heavier flavors we pair with duck.

Pro Notes and Tips

- I was inspired by traditional Italian preparations in the creation of this dish, in particular, gremolata and agrodolce.

- If nutty, fragrant chanterelle mushrooms are not available, substitute delicate oyster mushrooms.

TOMATO-GINGER AGRODOLCE

- 2 tablespoons (25 grams) granulated sugar
- 1 tablespoon (15 grams) water
- 1 tomato, coarsely chopped
- 1 tablespoon (10 grams) ginger, minced
- 2 tablespoons (20 grams) dried cherries, chopped
- 1 tablespoon (15 grams) white wine vinegar
- 3 cups (720 grams) chicken or duck stock
  salt, to taste

1. Place the sugar and the water in a small saucepan and carefully cook to a light caramel. Remove from the heat and add the tomato, ginger, dried cherries, and vinegar.

2. Return to medium heat and add the chicken stock. Continue to cook, reducing the liquid by one-third. Strain the sauce, pressing on the solids to extract as much liquid as possible, and season to taste with salt. Reserve warm.

FENNEL-APPLE PURÉE

- 2 tablespoons (25 grams) granulated sugar
- 1 tablespoon (15 grams) water
- ¼ teaspoon (0.5 gram) cinnamon powder
- 1 Granny Smith apple, peeled, cored, and coarsely chopped
- ½ fennel bulb, rinsed, cored, and thinly sliced
  white wine or water, as needed
- 2 teaspoons (10 grams) olive oil
  salt, to taste

1. Place the sugar and the water in a small saucepan and carefully cook to a light caramel. Remove from heat and add the cinnamon, apple, and fennel.

2. Add white wine to barely cover the apple and fennel and return to low heat, cooking until the mixture is softened and most of the water has evaporated.

3. Transfer the mixture to a blender. Add the olive oil, and purée until very smooth. Pass through a fine mesh strainer. Season with salt to taste and reserve warm.

SEARED DUCK BREAST

2-3 medium duck breasts, trimmed, skin side scored
    salt, to taste
  1 cinnamon stick
    sage leaves, as needed

1. Preheat a large sauté pan over medium heat. Season the duck breasts on both sides with salt and place them into the pan, skin side down. Continue to cook over medium heat to gently render the fat without burning the skin.

2. As the duck cooks, occasionally drain some of the excess fat and reserve for the other preparations.

3. Once the skin has nicely browned (after about 5 minutes), flip the duck breasts over and remove from heat. Place the cinnamon stick and a few sage leaves into the pan, and put into an oven preheated to 400°F (205°C) to continue cooking the duck to desired doneness (for medium rare, about 5 additional minutes).

4. Remove the duck from the oven and rest for 5 to 10 minutes while finishing and assembling the dish.

CHANTERELLE MUSHROOMS

18-24 medium chanterelle mushrooms, cleaned, and trimmed
      reserved fat from seared duck breast
      salt, to taste

1. While the seared duck breast rests, gently sauté the mushrooms in the reserved fat until lightly browned.

2. Remove from heat and season with salt to taste. Reserve warm.

GREMOLATA

  2 tablespoons (15 grams) apple, fine brunoise
  2 tablespoons (15 grams) celery, cut into thin cross-sections
  1 tablespoon (10 grams) Niçoise or Kalamata olives, fine brunoise
  2 tablespoons (20 grams) dried cherries, finely chopped

1. Combine the apple, celery, olives, and cherries and toss to combine. Reserve.

TO SERVE

  reserved fat from seared duck breast
  Maldon salt, as needed
  micro basil leaves
  fennel tops
  celery leaves

1. Brush the rested duck breasts with some of the reserved duck fat, and season with salt. Slice the duck breasts on a long diagonal bias. Arrange the sliced duck on warmed plates.

2. Arrange the gremolata mixture on the top of the slices, followed by the herbs and the sautéed mushrooms.

3. Apply a dollop of the fennel and apple purée to the plate and spoon the agrodolce around the duck breast. Serve immediately.

Czech Pork Belly Moussaka

This may be one of our best-known recipes—not because a reporter from *The New Yorker* was in the room when it was created, but because of the outrageous mix of ingredients. This dish was universally met with skepticism, which persisted until people tasted it. In the end, I think it proves how Chef Watson can push humans to work outside their comfort zones. Celery root, peas, red pepper, and dill make a truly memorable combination.

Pro Notes and Tips

- To create even layers, first line a baking pan with plastic wrap. Add half of the pea mixture to the pan and spread into an even layer. Then layer in the pork belly, and top with the remaining vegetables and a second layer of the pork belly. Cover the entire pan with plastic wrap, press gently, and refrigerate the pan overnight to set the layers.

- When ready to serve, spread the parsley root mousse over the top of the dish, top with cheese, and broil until well browned.

- If needed, celery root is an appropriate substitute for parsley root.

PORK BELLY SOUS VIDE

2.2	pounds (1,000 grams) pork belly
	kosher salt
	pepper, freshly ground

1. Preheat the oven to 325°F (160°C).

2. Season the pork belly with salt and pepper. Place on a rack and roast, covered, for 3 hours.

3. Increase the heat to 450°F (232°C) and continue cooking, uncovered, until well browned. Remove and cool completely before slicing.

Alternatively: Season the pork with salt and pepper, vacuum seal in a heat-safe bag, and cook in a water bath at 162°F (72°C) for 18 to 24 hours. Remove meat from bag and sear on the stove. Cool completely before slicing.

PARSLEY ROOT PURÉE

2	tablespoons (25 grams) butter
½	pound (225 grams) parsley root, diced
1½	cups (350 grams) milk
⅜	cup (75 grams) cottage cheese

1. Heat the butter in a pressure cooker over medium-high heat. Add the parsley root and cook briefly. Add the milk and place a lid on the pressure cooker. Bring the pot to high pressure (15 psi) and cook 10 minutes. Release the pressure from the pot.

2. Transfer the mixture to a blender. Add the cottage cheese and process until smooth. Reserve.

VEGETABLE MIXTURE

2	tablespoons (28 grams) butter
½	cup (120 grams) celery root, peeled, and brunoise
¼	cup (60 grams) red pepper, peeled, and small-diced
½	cup (120 grams) green peas, blanched, and shocked
1	cup (225 grams) parsley root purée
2	teaspoons (5 grams) fresh dill, chopped
½	cup (60 grams) Swiss cheese, grated

1. Melt the butter in a large sauté pan over high heat. Add the celery root and sauté 1 to 2 minutes to soften, but do not brown. Add the peppers and sauté until both vegetables are tender, 2 to 3 minutes more.

2. When the vegetables are tender, add the peas, parsley root purée, and dill. Simmer together briefly, then remove from the heat and stir in the cheese.

PARSLEY ROOT MOUSSE

- 1 cup (225 grams) parsley root purée
- 1 tablespoon (10 grams) flour
- 1 egg yolk

1. Blend the parsley root purée, flour, and egg yolk until smooth. Transfer to a siphon, and add 2 cartridges of gas.

TO SERVE

- ½ cup (65 grams) cheddar cheese, grated

1. Cut the pork belly into ½- to ¾-inch (1¼- to 2-cm) slices.

2. Spread half of the vegetable mixture into the base of an ovenproof baking dish. Layer slices of pork over the vegetables. Then repeat the layers, finishing with the pork belly. Dispense the parsley root mousse on top of the pork belly, then scatter the grated cheese over the dish. Cook under a broiler until well browned.

Kenyan Brussels Sprouts

While it is not uncommon, cardamom is a spice I rarely use in my cooking. I typically associate it with other baking spices like cinnamon, nutmeg, and clove. The challenge here was to pair the spice with the earthy flavor profile of Brussels sprouts and celery.

CHEF WATSON SAYS

SURPRISE   PLEASANTNESS   SYNERGY

Pro Notes and Tips

- Placing the purée in a specially made canister and injecting it with nitrous oxide (N_2O) gives the sweet potatoes a light, mousse-like texture. Whipping canisters are an essential tool in the modern kitchen. They can be used to lighten vegetable purées (as in this recipe), to instantly make whipped cream, or to infuse liquids, creating anything from flavored alcohols to pickle in a matter of seconds.

- After draining the blanched Brussels sprouts, spread on a sheet pan to let them steam dry.

SWEET POTATO PURÉE

- 6 cloves garlic (30 grams), chopped
- 1 piece fresh ginger (80 grams), minced
- 2 celery stalks (60 grams), thinly sliced
- 2 sweet potatoes (500 grams), peeled, and chopped
  black pepper, to taste
  kosher salt, to taste

1. Combine the garlic, ginger, and celery, and sweat in olive oil until aromatic. Add sweet potatoes and cook 5 minutes. Add enough water to cover. Simmer until tender.

2. Purée smooth in a high powered blender and season with salt and pepper. Optional: Transfer purée to whipping canister and charge with 2 N_2O cartridges.

CRISPY SPICED BRUSSELS

- 1 pound (500 grams) Brussels sprouts, halved
- 2 teaspoons (5 grams) cardamom
- 1 teaspoon (2 grams) ginger, ground
  black pepper, to taste
  kosher salt, to taste
  oil, as needed

1. Bring a large pot of salted water to a boil. Blanch the Brussels sprouts 2 minutes. Drain.

2. Heat a pot of oil to 375°F (190°C). Fry the Brussels sprouts in small batches. When golden brown, remove and toss with spices and salt.

ALMOND GREMOLATA

- 1 tablespoon (8 grams) almonds, toasted, and coarsely chopped
- 1 tablespoon (6 grams) celery leaves, minced
- 1 tablespoon (6 grams) parsley, minced
- 2 teaspoons (4 grams) garlic, minced
  kosher salt, to taste

1. Combine all ingredients. Mix well and season with salt.

TO SERVE

1. Spoon some of the purée into a small dish. Top with crispy Brussels sprouts and almond gremolata.

Russian Beet Salad

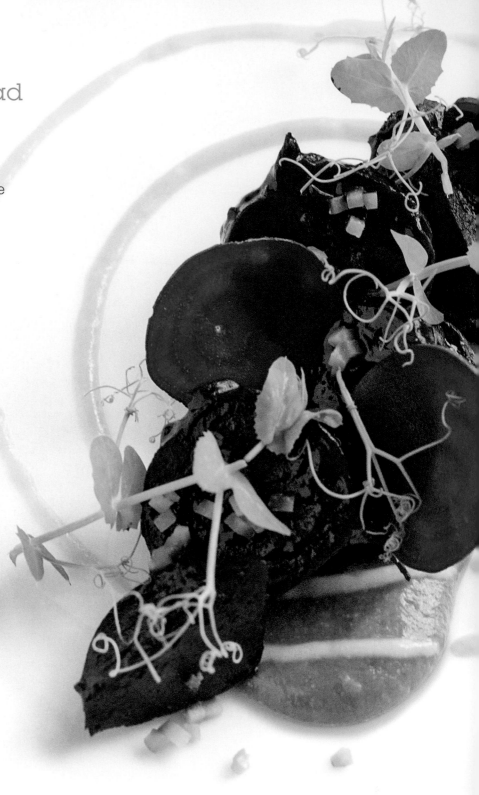

Prunes and pickles, need I say more? This unusual list of ingredients presents a challenge at every turn. While there are some traditional pairings like tomato, cucumber, and basil, discovering a molecular connection between beets, prunes, and pickles was particularly unexpected. Together the balance of sweet, tart, and earthy makes each bite more interesting than the last.

CHEF WATSON SAYS

SURPRISE   PLEASANTNESS   **SYNERGY**

Pro Notes and Tips

• Roasted yellow tomato coulis gives this dish brilliant color. If you cannot locate yellow tomatoes, substitute yellow bell peppers.

ROASTED BEET AND PRUNE PURÉE

18   baby red beets
½   cup (100 grams) prunes
3   tablespoons (45 grams) butter
2   tablespoons (25 grams) basil stems
½   cup (120 grams) red wine vinegar
1   teaspoon (5 grams) salt
     pinch ground black pepper

1. Combine all ingredients in a small roasting pan. Cover tightly with foil, and roast in a 350°F (175°C) oven for 1 hour or until completely tender. Let cool for a few minutes.

2. Peel the beets and reserve.

3. Discard the basil stems. Transfer the remaining ingredients to a blender and purée until smooth. Add water to adjust consistency as needed.

CUCUMBER AND HERB COULIS

1   cup (60 grams) basil leaves
1   cup (60 grams) parsley leaves
½   cup (150 grams) canned white beans, drained
1   pound (500 grams) cucumber, seeded, and chopped
     salt, to taste

1. Bring a large pot of salted water to a boil. Add the herbs and cook until completely tender (3 to 4 minutes). Refresh in ice water. Squeeze dry when cooled.

2. Place the beans in a small saucepan and cover completely with cold water. Bring to a boil and cook 1 minute. Drain and set aside to cool.

3. Combine the squeezed herbs, cooled beans, and cucumbers in a blender and process until smooth. Season to taste with salt.

ROASTED TOMATO PURÉE

2.2   pounds (1,000 grams) yellow tomato
     salt and pepper, to taste

1. Cut the tomatoes in half and lay them, flat side down, on a baking sheet. Roast in a 500°F (260°C) oven until the skins darken and pull away from the flesh (about 20 to 30 minutes). Remove from the oven and let cool.

2. Squeeze the tomatoes to remove the seeds and discard the skins. Transfer the mixture to a blender and process until smooth. Season to taste with salt and pepper.

TO SERVE

2   tablespoons (20 grams) cornichon, minced
     micro basil, as needed
     cucumber and pea tendrils

1. Cut the beets and dress with the prune purée.

2. Spread a thin layer of the cucumber coulis on the base of a plate. Drizzle with some of the tomato purée.

3. Spoon the beets into the center of the plate and garnish with the cornichon, micro basil, and tendrils.

Ecuadorian Strawberry Dessert

With this dessert, I hoped to preserve the ingredients' fresh fruit flavors, but present them in unexpected ways. I also wanted to channel dessert traditions of Latin America through contemporary and classic pastry techniques.

CHEF WATSON SAYS

SURPRISE   PLEASANTNESS   SYNERGY

Pro Notes and Tips

- Because the alginate spherification technique used to create the liquid-filled orbs of strawberry requires extra patience and ingredients (there are several online sources for the calcium lactate, sodium alginate, and sodium citrate), one can easily substitute simple chopped or puréed strawberries to add texture and flavor to the dish.

DULCE DE COCO

¼ cup (85 grams) dulce de leche
2 tablespoons (20 grams) coconut milk

1. Place the dulce de leche in a small mixing bowl and slowly whisk in the coconut milk to create a spreadable consistency. Reserve chilled.

STRAWBERRY WATER

8 ounces (225 grams) strawberries, roughly chopped
3 tablespoons (40 grams) granulated sugar

1. Combine the strawberries and sugar in a large bowl. Cover and place in a warm area and let stand for up to 6 hours.

2. Transfer to refrigeration and chill, at least 4 hours or overnight. Strain the mixture, discarding the solids.

PAPAYA-APPLE SALAD

½ cup (100 grams) papaya, diced into small cubes
½ cup (50 grams) dried apple, diced into small cubes
½ cup (125 grams) strawberry water
   finely ground coriander, to taste
   finely ground cumin, to taste

1. Toss all of the ingredients together and allow to stand for 2 hours to fully hydrate the dried apple.

CHOUX SABLÉE

¼ cup (55 grams) unsalted butter, softened
¼ cup (65 grams) granulated sugar
⅔ cup (65) grams all purpose flour
   pinch (1 gram) fine sea salt

1. Place all of the ingredients into the bowl of a stand mixer fitted with a paddle. Mix on low speed just until combined, adding a small amount of water if necessary.

2. Roll the dough into a thin sheet, between 2 sheets of parchment paper cut to about 6- by 8-inches (15- by 20-centimeters). Freeze.

3. Using a ring cutter, cut the sablée dough into 1-inch (3-centimeter) discs.

AVOCADO OIL CHOUX

- 5 tablespoons (70 grams) whole milk
- 4 tablespoons (60 grams) water
- 1 teaspoon (5 grams) granulated sugar
  pinch (1 gram) salt
- 2 tablespoons (30 grams) unsalted butter
- 1 tablespoon plus 1 teaspoon (20 grams) avocado oil
- 5 tablespoons (45 grams) all purpose flour
- 3 tablespoons (30 grams) bread flour
- 2 eggs (about 110 grams)

1. Place the milk, water, sugar, salt, butter, and avocado oil in a saucepan and bring to a rolling boil.

2. Remove from heat and stir in the all purpose and bread flours until combined. Return to heat and cook for 1 to 2 minutes until a smooth mass has formed.

3. Transfer the cooked mixture to the bowl of a stand mixer fitted with a paddle attachment. Beat the mixture until slightly cooled. Incorporate the eggs one at a time, scraping down the bowl after each addition.

4. Transfer the paste to a pastry bag and deposit into 1-inch (3-centimeter) diameter silicone half sphere forms (the recipe will yield about 36 pieces). Freeze.

5. Unmold and arrange the frozen half spheres onto 2 parchment-lined baking pans, allowing ample space between rows. Top each half sphere with a disc of the cut choux sablée. Temper to room temperature.

6. Place in an oven preheated to 340°F (170°C) and bake for 5 minutes. Reduce the heat to 320°F (160°C) and continue to bake an additional 5 minutes. Reduce the heat to 300°F (150°C) and finish baking until golden and dry, about 10 minutes.

COCONUT PASTRY CREAM

- 1 cup (210 grams) coconut milk
- ½ cup (120 grams) whole milk
- ½ cup (105 grams) heavy cream
- ½ cup (60 grams) confectioners sugar
- 2 tablespoons (15 grams) all purpose flour
- 3 egg yolks (about 60 grams)
- 1 leaf sheet gelatin, bloomed in cold water
- 1 tablespoon (15 grams) unsalted butter, softened

1. Place the coconut milk, whole milk, and cream in a heavy saucepan and bring to a boil.

2. Sift together the confectioners sugar and flour.

3. In three additions, whisk the dry ingredients into the egg yolks. Temper the hot coconut milk mixture into the eggs and return to medium heat.

4. Stirring constantly, continue to cook until the mixture is thickened and returns to a boil.

5. Remove from heat and add the gelatin. Transfer the mixture to a stand mixer bowl fitted with a paddle attachment. Beat until cool, adding in the softened butter.

6. Pour into a shallow container, cover with plastic wrap, and chill.

ALGINATE BATH

- 4 cups (1,000 grams) water
- 2½ teaspoons (7 grams) sodium alginate
- ¼ teaspoon (2 grams) sodium citrate
- 2 cups (500 grams) simple syrup (60% water, 40% granulated sugar)

1. Shear the water, sodium alginate, and sodium citrate together with an immersion blender for at least 2 minutes and allow to fully hydrate for 2 hours.

2. Drop the frozen strawberry forms (recipe follows) into the alginate bath and allow to set for 3 to 4 minutes. Gently transfer to a clean water bath and then into the syrup for holding.

STRAWBERRY SPHERES

1	cup (200 grams) strawberry purée
1½	teaspoons (5 grams) calcium lactate
	pinch (0.5 gram) xanthan gum (optional)

1. Thoroughly whisk or blend the ingredients together. Divide the mixture into 1 inch (3 cm) half sphere forms and freeze.

PEACH YOGURT SORBET

¾	cup (140 grams) granulated sugar
⅓	cup (75 grams) water
2	cups (480 grams) white peach purée
1¼	cup (320 grams) plain whole milk yogurt

1. Combine the sugar and water in a small saucepan and heat just until the sugar has dissolved. Remove from the heat and cool.

2. Combine the syrup, peach purée, and yogurt. Process in an ice cream machine according to the manufacturer's instructions. Reserve the sorbet in the freezer.

PEACH COULIS

½	cup (125 grams) white peach purée
2	tablespoons (25 grams) granulated sugar
1	teaspoon (2.5 grams) apple pectin powder

1. Place the peach purée into a small saucepan and bring to a gentle boil.

2. Combine the sugar and pectin, and whisk into the purée. Resume a boil, remove from heat, and cool.

TO SERVE

Confectioners sugar, as needed

1. Fill 18 choux puffs with the coconut pastry cream and dust with confectioners sugar.

2. Arrange 3 puffs on each of 6 plates and artfully garnish with the remaining components: dulce de coco, peach coulis, papaya salad, and strawberry spheres. Finish with a scoop of the peach yogurt sorbet. Serve immediately.

Ivorian Bourbon Punch

The challenges here went beyond balancing the diverse flavors. With an ample amount of fruit ingredients, I had to create a cocktail that didn't feel like a smoothie. I came upon a method of making our own turmeric-infused banana juice that used amylase to convert the fruit's starch into sugar. The juice was delicious and not too thick, but the process took nearly 4 hours. Finally we tracked down bottled banana juice, which led to the recipe here.

—JAMES BRISCIONE

CHEF WATSON SAYS

SURPRISE   PLEASANTNESS   SYNERGY

Pro Notes and Tips

• For the best consistency, combine the turmeric, lemon and lime juices and honey, prior to incorporating other ingredients, and stir well until the turmeric and honey are dissolved.

PREPARATION

- 8 ounces banana juice
- 2 ounces bourbon
- 1 ounce triple sec
- 1½ teaspoons vanilla extract
- 1½ teaspoons ground turmeric
- ½ ounce lemon juice
- ½ ounce lime juice
- 1 teaspoon honey

1. Combine all the ingredients in a cocktail shaker and stir until the honey and turmeric are dissolved.

2. Fill a shaker with ice and shake until well chilled. Pour over ice and garnish with a lemon slice.

  SERVES 4   2 MINUTES

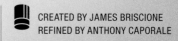 CREATED BY JAMES BRISCIONE
REFINED BY ANTHONY CAPORALE

4 Dueling Dishes

In the early days of cognitive cooking, the Chef Watson team toured a series of IBM events, from analyst conferences to press gatherings—even a Canadian Poutine Challenge. (Look for these recipes from ICE Chefs Sabrina Sexton and Michael Garrett.) In many cases, the participants got a chance to interact with the system and contribute to the recipes in this chapter. Early experiments also led to a variety of

"dueling dish" pairs: two different recipes created from the same list of ingredients.

In one instance, preparing for the Falling Walls conference in Berlin, Chef Watson and a group of German chefs instructed the system to focus on Spanish, American, Asian, and German regional cuisines. Chefs then created a dozen new concoctions and served them to a dinner crowd of 400—a major undertaking.

At another gathering at the Institute of Culinary Education, about 50 students suggested inputs that led to a Cuban bouillabaisse. Chef Watson produced the ingredients, including squash, jalapeño, plantain, and lobster. ICE Chefs, Michael Laiskonis and James Briscione, then raced against the clock to prepare two different and delicious dishes. Try them out and compare.

For a *Food & Wine* magazine article, Chef Watson was challenged to combine two distinct culinary traditions, Jewish and Thai. The result blends asparagus, banana, brown rice, pickle, and garlic, among many other ingredients. Here's betting it's like nothing anyone has eaten before, and it also comes in two versions, one from each ICE chef.

BEEF FLANK, PAPRIKA, DRIED
SAVORY, RICE VINEGAR, TOM
BAMBOO SHOOTS, COCONUT

Filipino Tomato Salad

"We thought looking at a tomato salad in the context of the Pacific Islands was a fun idea, matching a region and an ingredient you don't typically see together. Since creating this, the coconut dressing has become my favorite topping for ripe tomatoes."

—JAMES BRISCIONE

"We paired 'Filipino' with 'tomato' to see what Watson would come up with. The deeply flavored, umami-rich shrimp paste emerged as the key harmonizing element.**"**

—MICHAEL LAISKONIS

James' Filipino Tomato Salad

As we created this dish, a film crew from FOX NY was in the kitchen with the cameras rolling. We thought looking at a tomato salad in the context of the Pacific Islands was a fun idea, matching a region and an ingredient you don't typically see together. Since creating this, the coconut dressing has become my favorite topping for ripe tomatoes. The richness of the coconut and spicy umami of the shrimp paste are indescribably delicious—meaning you must make it to taste it for yourself.

CHEF WATSON SAYS

SURPRISE   PLEASANTNESS   SYNERGY

Pro Notes and Tips

- Shrimp paste, a typical ingredient in Southeast Asian cuisines, is made from ground-up fermented shrimp.

- We chose a shrimp paste ground with garlic and chiles. If you cannot find shrimp paste, a mixture of fish sauce and Sriracha is an adequate substitute (use them in a ratio of 2:1, respectively).

GRILLED FLANK STEAK
- 1   piece (28 grams) lemongrass, thinly sliced
- 2   sprigs savory, chopped
- 1   tablespoon (20 grams) shrimp paste
- 1   dried red chile
- 2   tablespoons (28 grams) annatto oil
- 1   pound (454 grams) flank steak, sliced

1. Combine the lemongrass, savory, shrimp paste, chile powder, annatto oil, and rice vinegar in a bowl and mix well. Add the beef and toss well to coat.

2. When ready to serve, brush excess marinade from steak and season lightly with salt. Grill 6 minutes per side or to desired doneness. Rest on rack before slicing.

COCONUT DRESSING
- 1   cup (235 grams) coconut milk
- 1   scant tablespoon (16 grams) shrimp paste
      ground red chile, to taste (optional)

1. Combine all of the ingredients in a bowl and whisk until smooth. Season to taste with chile and salt.

TOMATO BRINE
- ½   cup (115 grams) rice vinegar
- 1   teaspoon shrimp paste
- 1   (4 grams) dried red chile, crushed
- 1   pound (454 grams) heirloom tomatoes, cut into bite-sized pieces

1. In a shallow pan, whisk together the rice vinegar, shrimp paste, and chile.

2. Add the tomatoes, mix gently to coat, and set aside to marinate until ready to plate.

GRILLED CELERY
- 4   ribs celery

1. Peel the celery and cut in half lengthwise to create flat pieces. Brush the celery with the coconut dressing and grill until lightly charred. Reserve for plating.

FRIED BAMBOO SHOOTS

20 slices bamboo shoot
   kosher salt, as needed
   paprika, as needed

1. Dry bamboo shoots well on paper towels. Fry in 350°F (175°C) oil until brown and crisp. Drain on paper towels and season with salt and paprika. Reserve for plating.

SPINACH

1 tablespoon (15 grams) annatto oil
1 dried arbol chile
2 cups (80 grams) spinach leaves

1. Heat oil in a sauté pan with chile. When the chile begins to sizzle, add the spinach and sauté briefly. Do not wilt completely. Drain on paper towels and reserve for plating.

TO SERVE

celery leaves
micro celery

1. Spread some of the coconut dressing across the base of a plate. Place a few piles of spinach and tomatoes on top of the dressing, adding some of the sliced beef and grilled celery.

2. Finish the plate by adding the fried bamboo shoots, celery leaf, and micro celery.

Michael's Filipino Tomato Salad

The goal was to demonstrate how two chefs might interpret the same list of ingredients in different ways — or, as we discovered, how they might approach a single output in a similar way. When we paired "Filipino" with "tomato" to see what Watson would come up with, the deeply flavored, umami-rich shrimp paste emerged as the key harmonizing element.

Pro Notes and Tips

- Flank steak is a juicy and flavorful cut that works well for this room-temperature salad.

- Take care to avoid overcooking the meat, and, once it's properly rested, be sure to slice against the grain for optimum tenderness.

FLANK STEAK

- ½ cup (120 grams) coconut water
- 2 tablespoons (25 grams) shrimp paste
- 1 teaspoon (2 grams) smoked paprika
- 1 teaspoon (1 gram) red pepper flakes
- ½ tablespoon (15 grams) annatto oil
- ½ teaspoon (3 grams) fine sea salt
- 4 branches savory
- 1½ pounds (675 grams) flank steak
  fine sea salt, as needed

1. Combine the coconut water, shrimp paste, paprika, red pepper flakes, annatto oil, and salt in a small mixing bowl and whisk to combine. Place the mixture, along with the savory and flank steak, in a large zip-seal bag and refrigerate for at least 8 hours or overnight.

2. Remove the flank steak from the bag and discard the marinade. Season the steak with salt on both sides and place on a preheated grill, cooking for 3 to 4 minutes on each side or to a doneness of medium rare.

3. Remove the steak from the grill and transfer to a cutting board; rest the meat for 5 to 10 minutes before slicing. Once rested, thinly slice the steak against the grain and reserve for assembly.

LEMONGRASS-PICKLED CELERY

- ½ cup (55 grams) celery, thinly sliced
- ½ teaspoon (5 grams) granulated sugar
- ½ teaspoon (3 grams) fine sea salt
- ¼ cup (60 grams) coconut water
- ½ cup (120 grams) rice vinegar
- 1 stalk lemongrass, cut into 2-inch (5-centimeter) sections, and bruised

1. To lightly blanch the celery, bring a small saucepan of water to a boil. Remove from the heat and add the sliced celery. Allow to stand for a few seconds and drain. Transfer to a bowl of cold water to halt the cooking process and drain again.

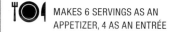 MAKES 6 SERVINGS AS AN APPETIZER, 4 AS AN ENTRÉE    40 MINUTES, PLUS MARINATING AND PICKLING    MICHAEL LAISKONIS

2. Place the blanched celery in a small jar or lidded container. Meanwhile, place all of the remaining ingredients in a small saucepan and bring to a simmer, stirring to dissolve the salt and sugar.

3. Remove from heat and add the coconut water-vinegar mixture and lemongrass into the container with the celery. Allow to cool at room temperature and then refrigerate for at least 30 minutes or up to 8 hours (the pickled celery will also keep in the refrigerator for up to a week or more).

TOMATO SALAD

- 1 teaspoon (4 grams) shrimp paste
- 1 teaspoon (1 gram) savory, finely chopped
- ½ teaspoon (1 gram) smoked paprika
- 2 teaspoons (10 grams) rice vinegar
- 2 tablespoons (30 grams) extra virgin olive oil
- 2 medium ripe plum or heirloom tomatoes (about 225 grams), sliced or cut into bite-sized pieces
- 2 medium ripe yellow tomatoes (about 225 grams), sliced or cut into bite-sized pieces
- ¼ cup (50 grams) canned bamboo shoots, thinly sliced
- fine sea salt, to taste

1. Place the shrimp paste, savory, paprika, rice vinegar, and olive oil in a small mixing bowl, and whisk to combine. Add the tomatoes and bamboo shoots. Toss well to combine and season with salt, as desired.

WILTED SPINACH

- 1 tablespoon (15 grams) extra virgin olive oil
- 3 cups loosely packed young spinach (90 grams)
- red pepper flakes, to taste
- fine sea salt, to taste

1. Heat the olive oil in a large sauté pan over medium heat and add the spinach. Quickly stir the spinach, seasoning with red pepper flakes and salt, until lightly wilted. Remove from the heat and cool.

TO SERVE

- coarse sea salt, to taste

1. Arrange the sliced flank steak onto each plate. Top the steak with several pieces of the pickled celery, some of the tomato salad, and the wilted spinach. Spoon some additional liquid from the tomato salad over the plate and finish with a sprinkle of coarse sea salt.

Fennel-Saffron Risotto

The original version of this dish, served at Berlin's Falling Walls conference, included an inventive pairing of hot risotto with a contrasting frozen martini granité. In revisiting the risotto, I chose to incorporate the classic gin and vermouth into the risotto itself. The surprise—and challenge—here is the candied ginger. We had to tame its sweetness and integrate its heat, both providing an interesting foil to the richness of the other ingredients.

—MICHAEL LAISKONIS

CHEF WATSON SAYS

SURPRISE PLEASANTNESS SYNERGY

Pro Notes and Tips

- A successful risotto requires starchy, short grain rice like Arborio or carnaroli.

- The proper loose and creamy consistency is achieved by the slow incorporation of the hot broth or stock and constant stirring.

OVEN-DRIED CHERRY TOMATOES

    2 cups (300 grams) small cherry tomatoes, cleaned, and halved
    1 tablespoon (15 grams) extra virgin olive oil
       fine sea salt, as needed

1. Arrange the tomato halves, cut side up, on a parchment or Silpat-lined sheet pan. Drizzle with the oil and lightly season with salt.

2. Place the tomatoes in an oven preheated to 200°F (93°C) and slowly dry for 2 to 3 hours (until slightly shriveled). Do not allow the tomatoes to brown.

3. Remove the tomatoes from the oven and cool. Reserve for final assembly.

VEGETABLE BROTH

    ½ cup (65 grams) carrots, peeled, and diced
    ½ cup (55 grams) celery, diced
    ½ cup (60 grams) leeks, white portion only, cleaned, and diced
    5 cups (1,200 grams) water

   SERVES ABOUT 6   45 MINUTES, PLUS OVEN-DRYING    CREATED BY SARAH WIENER
REFINED BY MICHAEL LAISKONIS

1. Combine the vegetables and water in a medium-size saucepan. Bring to a boil, reduce heat to low, and simmer for 5 minutes.

2. Remove the saucepan from heat. Cover and allow the broth to stand for 20 minutes. Drain the broth through a strainer, discard the vegetables, and reserve the broth for the final assembly.

TO SERVE

  5 cups (1,200 grams) vegetable broth
  2 pinches saffron threads, crushed
  6 tablespoons (70 grams) unsalted butter, divided
  ½ cup (60 grams) onion, diced
  ½ cup (65 grams) fennel, diced
1½ cups (320 grams) Arborio or carnaroli rice
  1 tablespoon (15 grams) dry vermouth
  2 tablespoons (30 grams) gin
  2 tablespoons (25 grams) candied ginger, finely chopped
  ½ cup (120 grams) olive oil
  ¼ cup (5 grams) parsley leaves

  ½ cup (50 grams) Parmigiano-Reggiano cheese, grated (or more, if desired)
  2 tablespoons (4 grams) fresh flat-leaf parsley, chopped
     fine sea salt, to taste
     freshly ground black pepper, to taste

1. Place vegetable broth and saffron in a saucepan and bring to a gentle simmer over medium heat. Reduce heat to the lowest setting to keep the broth warm.

2. Heat 2 tablespoons of butter in a large saucepan over medium heat and add the onion and fennel, stirring occasionally. Sweat until softened (3 to 4 minutes). Add the rice and continue to cook for 2 to 3 minutes, stirring to coat the rice with butter. Add the vermouth and gin, stirring until the liquid is completely absorbed (2 minutes).

3. Reduce the heat slightly and begin adding the warm vegetable broth, about 1 cup (225 grams) at a time, stirring frequently after each addition. Continue to cook until absorbed before the next addition of broth.

4. While the rice is cooking, combine the reserved dried tomatoes, candied ginger, and 1 tablespoon of butter in a separate pan, gently heating until warmed, tossing to combine.

5. In a third saucepan, heat the olive oil to 350°F (175°C). Add the parsley leaves and gently fry for 5 to 10 seconds. Remove the parsley from the oil with a slotted spoon and drain on a paper towel. Gently season with salt.

6. When all the liquid has been added and the rice is tender but slightly firm to the bite (about 20 minutes), stir in 3 tablespoons of butter, grated cheese, and parsley. Season with salt and pepper. (The finished rice should be fairly loose, with a creamy consistency).

7. To serve, spoon risotto into shallow bowls and top with warmed tomato mixture and fried parsley leaves.

SAFFRON, LOBSTER, BAY JALAPEÑO, MINT, OLIVE SHRIMP, ONION, GINGER,

Cuban Lobster Bouillabaisse

" As Michael and I created our own unique versions of this dish live in front of a crowd, the pressure was truly on. Not only did we have to squeeze distinctly Latin ingredients into an iconic Mediterranean dish, but we also had to create the recipe in real time, with no time to plan."

—JAMES BRISCIONE

LEAF, CUCUMBER, CHIVE, OIL, PLANTAIN, SQUASH, OREGANO, CORIANDER

"With suggestions from an audience of ICE students, an output was created and we immediately began cooking, without much time to plot a strategy. With this dish, Latin meets Mediterranean, and I chose to transform bouillabaisse—a traditional fish stew—into a cold or room temperature salad."

—MICHAEL LAISKONIS

Michael's Cuban Lobster Bouillabaisse

This dish was the first live challenge attempted with the system: a real-time demonstration in front of an audience. With suggestions from an audience of ICE students, an output was created and we immediately began cooking, without much time to plot a strategy. With this dish, Latin meets Mediterranean, and I chose to transform bouillabaisse— a traditional fish stew—into a cold or room temperature salad.

CHEF WATSON SAYS

SURPRISE   PLEASANTNESS   SYNERGY

Pro Notes and Tips

- The caviar-like effect of the cucumber pearls is worth the time and effort, but they can be replaced with a diced or julienned cucumber.

- Though gelled in this recipe, the saffron broth would make a wonderful base for a warm dish.

- This chilled dish makes a great light lunch or first course, but feel free to adjust the portion size for a heartier main course.

SAFFRON BROTH

- 8   pieces large shrimp (about 225 grams), shell-on
- ½   small onion (75 grams), diced
- 1½   teaspoon (7 grams) ginger, peeled, and finely minced
- 1   teaspoon (1 gram) coriander seeds
- 1   small plum tomato (about 100 grams), diced
- 1   sprig fresh oregano
       pinch saffron threads
- 2   cups (450 grams) water
       fine sea salt, to taste
- 3   leaves sheet gelatin, bloomed in cold water
       olive oil, as needed

1. Peel and devein the shrimp, reserving the shells. In a medium-size saucepan, heat a small amount of oil and add the shells, onion, ginger, and coriander seeds. Cook over low heat until shells have taken color and the aromatics become fragrant. Add the diced tomato, oregano, and saffron. Cook, stirring, for 2 minutes. Add water and bring to a boil. Reduce heat and simmer for 20 minutes.

2. Remove broth from heat and strain over the shrimp; cover and allow to poach for 6 to 7 minutes.

3. Strain and return broth to saucepan and continue to heat and gently reduce to a volume of about 1 cup (225 grams). Season with salt and stir in softened gelatin. Pour into a flat shallow dish and chill until set (1 to 2 hours).

4. Once set, cut the saffron broth gel into cubes and reserve chilled.

CUCUMBER PEARLS

-      juice of 2 English cucumbers (150 grams)
- 1   teaspoon (5 grams) granulated sugar
       fine sea salt, to taste
- ¼   cup plus two tablespoons (100 grams) water
       scant ½ teaspoon (1.7 grams) agar
- ⅛   teaspoon (0.3 gram) locust bean gum
- 4   cups (1 liter) vegetable oil at 40°F (5°C)

1. To prepare base, combine cucumber juice, sugar, and salt to taste. Heat just enough to dissolve sugar. Reserve.

2. Disperse agar and locust bean gum with water in a small saucepan.

3. Bring mixture to a boil, reduce heat, and simmer for 1 to 2 minutes.

4. Remove from heat and incorporate into cucumber juice. Transfer to plastic squeeze bottle.

5. Slowly drop mixture into the cold vegetable oil, allowing 5 to 10 minutes for it to set, then drain. Reserve chilled.

BUTTERNUT SQUASH

1 cup (200 grams) butternut squash, large-diced
fine sea salt, to taste

1. Bring pot of salted water to a boil. Add squash and cook just until tender, about 2 minutes. Remove from heat, drain, and spread on a sheet pan to cool.

PLANTAIN CHIPS

vegetable or corn oil, as needed
½ plantain, peeled, very thinly sliced
fine sea salt, to taste

1. Fill a saucepan halfway with oil, and heat to 350°F (175°C).

2. Rinse plantain slices in cold water and pat dry on paper towels.

3. In small batches, carefully add plantain slices to oil and fry until golden brown (3 to 4 minutes). Remove from oil, drain on paper towels, and lightly season with salt.

TO SERVE

2 teaspoons (10 grams) lemon juice
2 tablespoons (30 grams) extra virgin olive oil
fine sea salt, to taste
2 lobster tails (each about 175 grams), cooked, and sliced
1 small jalapeño pepper (about 30 grams), thinly sliced
1 small bunch chives, cut into long pieces
1 small bunch mint leaves
1 small bunch cilantro leaves

1. Whisk together lemon juice and olive oil, and season with salt. Toss the sliced lobster tails and shrimp in the lemon mixture and arrange among 4 plates. Add the cucumber pearls, butternut squash cubes, and saffron broth gel to each plate. Garnish with a few pieces of sliced jalapeño, chives, mint, cilantro, and plantain chips.

James' Cuban Lobster Bouillabaisse

As Michael and I created our own unique versions of this dish live in front of a crowd, the pressure was truly on. Not only did we have to squeeze distinctly Latin ingredients into an iconic Mediterranean dish, but we also had to create the recipe in real time, with no time to plan. I couldn't imagine bouillabaisse without its distinctive saffron flavor, but in this version the broth gets a spicy kick from fresh jalapeño.

CHEF WATSON SAYS

SURPRISE   PLEASANTNESS   SYNERGY

Pro Notes and Tips

- When making the lobster stock, make sure the pot never comes to a rapid boil, as gently simmering is the key to beautiful, clear broth. If the stock does come out a little cloudy, strain it through a coffee filter and let the broth settle. Most of the bits that make the broth cloudy will settle to the bottom, and the clean liquid can be poured off.

LOBSTER AND BROTH

- 2 whole lobsters, each about 1½ pounds (700 grams)
- 2 tablespoons (28 grams) olive oil
- 1½ cups (225 grams) yellow onion, diced
- ½ head garlic (about 35 grams)
- 1 tablespoon (2 grams) fresh oregano leaves
- 8 cups (2,000 grams) water
- 1 tablespoon (8 grams) jalapeño, sliced
- 2 branches mint
- 1 tablespoon (4 grams) coriander seeds, toasted
- 1 tablespoon (8 grams) ginger root, chopped
- ½ teaspoon (0.4 gram) saffron threads

1. Separate the heads, tails, and claws of the lobsters. Keep the heads for the broth.

2. Bring a pot of salted water to a boil. Blanch the tails for 3 minutes and the claws for 4 minutes.

3. Transfer the tails and claws to a bowl of ice water and let cool. Shell the tails and claws and reserve.

4. In a separate pot, heat the olive oil. Add the lobster bodies to the pot and cook until the shells are bright red. Add the onions, garlic, and oregano to the pot. Sweat the vegetables over medium heat until tender, but not browned. Pour in the water and bring the mixture to a gentle simmer. Cook over low heat for 45 minutes.

5. Place the jalapeño, mint, coriander seeds, ginger, and saffron threads in a clean bowl. Strain the lobster broth through a fine mesh strainer lined with cheesecloth, directly into the bowl with the spices. Leave the broth to steep for 30 minutes, then strain again.

PICKLED CUCUMBER

- 1 jalapeño, minced
- ¼ cup (40 grams) yellow onion, thinly sliced
- 2 cups (454 grams) white wine vinegar
- ½ cup (115 grams) water
- 1 tablespoon (12 grams) kosher salt
- 1 cup (200 grams) sugar
- ¼ cup (8 grams) fresh mint leaves
- 1 hothouse cucumber, thinly sliced lengthwise

1. Combine the jalapeño, onion, vinegar, water, salt and sugar in a saucepot. Bring to a boil to completely dissolve all of the ingredients. Chill completely, add mint and cucumbers. Set aside for at least 1 hour before serving.

BUTTERNUT SQUASH

2	tablespoons (28 grams) olive oil
12	pieces butternut squash, tourned
2	branches fresh oregano
3	cloves garlic, smashed
	water, as needed

1. Heat the olive oil in a medium-size sauté pan. Add the squash, oregano, and garlic and sauté gently until tender. Add water to the pan, as needed, to prevent the squash from browning.

OLIVE OIL POWDER

½	cup (120 grams) extra virgin olive oil
1	tablespoon (8 grams) ginger, thinly sliced
2	cloves garlic, thinly sliced
1.3	ounces (36 grams) tapioca maltodextrin

1. Combine the oil, ginger, and garlic in a saucepot. Heat over a low flame until the garlic begins to bubble. Remove from heat and set aside to cool.

2. Transfer the oil to a food processor and add the tapioca maltodextrin. Run the food processor until a powder forms. Store the powder in the freezer until ready to serve.

TO SERVE

	micro mint, as needed
	chives, cut into baton, as needed
12	pieces plantain chips

1. Place a small amount of the saffron-lobster broth in a saucepot. Add the shelled lobster and gently rewarm the meat. Roll the slices of pickled cucumbers into coils.

2. Arrange half a lobster tail and 1 claw in a shallow bowl and add the butternut squash, pickled cucumbers, and plantain chips. Garnish with a few spoonfuls of the olive oil powder and the herbs. Pour ¼ cup (60 grams) of the clear broth into each bowl immediately before serving.

ASPARAGUS, GARLIC, ONION, VEGETABLE STOCK, VANILLA, PICKLE, GRATED COCONUT, BROWN RICE,

Thai-Jewish Chicken

" Jewish and Thai are two cuisines I never imagined putting together before. I made the tater tots as a fun and fancy take on latkes, while Thai flavors show up in the form of curry, basil, and coconut. "

—JAMES BRISCIONE

APPLE, CURRY PASTE, POTATO, BASIL, BANANA, CHICKEN, CILANTRO, BLACK PEPPER, CANOLA OIL, SALT

" For me, the outliers here are the banana and asparagus. I particularly like the many textures and flavors in this presentation, and I'd love to revisit them again! "

—MICHAEL LAISKONIS

Michael's Thai-Jewish Chicken

This was another head-to-head exercise between James and myself, requiring us to quickly think on our feet and complete a dish within about a half hour. For me, the outliers here are the banana and asparagus. I particularly like the many textures and flavors in this presentation, and I'd love to revisit them again!

CHEF WATSON SAYS

SURPRISE   PLEASANTNESS   **SYNERGY**

Pro Notes and Tips

- In the initial exercise, I chose to wrap the chicken with thin slices of potato, using a special rotary slicing machine from Japan. Lightly frying broad slices or a thin julienne of potato would be a simple substitute for this technique.

- In our kitchen, I was able to precook the chicken sous vide before wrapping it with the potato. Two easy alternatives would be a light sauté or roasting in an oven.

CHICKEN BREAST

  2 tablespoons (25 grams) yellow curry paste
  1 vanilla bean, split, and scraped
  1 tablespoons (15 grams) chicken or vegetable stock
  ½ teaspoon (3 grams) fine sea salt
  2 large boneless, skinless chicken breast halves
      (each 225 to 275 grams)

1. Place the curry paste, vanilla pulp (the pod can be discarded or saved for another use), stock, and salt into a small bowl and whisk to combine.

2. Carefully trim each chicken breast half and slice in half lengthwise. Divide the chicken pieces between 2 medium or 4 small vacuum bags. Add the curry marinade mixture to the bag and close using a vacuum sealer. Marinate the chicken for up to 8 hours in the refrigerator or cook immediately.

3. Using an immersion circulator, preheat a water bath to 140°F (60°C). Add the bagged chicken breast and cook for at least 60 minutes or up to 90 minutes. Remove the bags from the water bath and briefly shock in an ice water bath. Reserve for assembly.

PICKLED GREEN APPLE

  1 small Granny Smith apple (120 grams), peeled, cored, and diced
  2 tablespoons (25 grams) banana, peeled, and mashed
  ½ vanilla bean, split, and scraped
  ¾ teaspoon (4 grams) fine sea salt
  ¼ cup (60 grams) water
  ½ cup (120 grams) rice vinegar or white wine vinegar
  5 whole black peppercorns

1. Place the diced apple in a small jar or lidded container. Meanwhile, place all of the remaining ingredients in a small saucepan and bring to a simmer.

2. Remove from heat and add the water-vinegar mixture into the container with the apple. Allow to cool at room temperature, then refrigerate for at least 30 minutes.

GARLIC PURÉE

  3 heads of garlic, peeled
      whole milk, as needed
      fine sea salt, to taste
      freshly ground black pepper, to taste

1. Slice the garlic very thin and place in a saucepan. Cover with milk, bring to a boil, drain the milk, and repeat this blanching process 2 more times.

2. Cover the garlic cloves with milk a fourth time and bring to a simmer, cooking until completely tender.

3. Using a blender or a food processor, purée the garlic and some of the cooking liquid to a smooth consistency. Season with salt and pepper, and reserve warm.

FRIED BROWN RICE

  1 tablespoon (15 grams) vegetable oil
  ¼ cup (50 grams) onion, diced
  1 clove garlic, minced
  2 spears asparagus, woody stems removed, blanched, and thinly sliced
  ¼ cup (25 grams) shredded dried coconut
  2 cups (about 320 grams) cooked brown rice
      fine sea salt, to taste
      freshly ground black pepper, to taste
  2 tablespoons (30 grams) chicken or vegetable stock

1. Preheat a large sauté pan over medium heat and add the vegetable oil. Add the onion and cook until softened and lightly browned. Add the garlic and asparagus. Continue to cook, stirring, for 1 to 2 minutes.

2. Add the coconut and cooked rice to the pan, and toss to combine. Cook until heated through and season with salt and pepper. Reserve warm. If the mixture appears dry, add a little stock.

TO SERVE

    vegetable oil, as needed

1 to 2 large Idaho potatoes, peeled, and thinly sliced lengthwise

    basil leaves, as needed

    cilantro leaves, as needed

    shredded dried coconut, as needed

1 banana, peeled, and cut lengthwise into 4 rectangular slices

    granulated sugar, as needed

8 spears asparagus, woody stems removed, blanched, and sliced into bite-sized pieces

    coarse sea salt, to taste

1. Heat the vegetable oil to 300°F (150°C) in a wide, shallow saucepan. To par-cook the potato, gently dip each of the slices into the oil for about 10 seconds. Remove from the oil and drain on a paper towel.

2. Arrange each piece of cooked chicken onto a work surface. Place several small basil and cilantro leaves onto each and finish with a sprinkle of the dried coconut.

Carefully wrap each piece of chicken with a layer of blanched potato slices.

3. Heat a small amount of oil in a large sauté pan over medium heat. Gently place the potato-wrapped chicken into the pan, turning and cooking on all sides until the potato is lightly browned. Remove from heat, and add the asparagus spears to the pan. Transfer to a 350°F (175°C) oven and continue to cook for 5 minutes.

4. Meanwhile, arrange the banana slices on an unlined sheet pan, sprinkle with a small amount of sugar, and lightly caramelize the banana with a blowtorch.

5. To serve, place some of the fried rice onto each plate and top with the cooked potato-wrapped chicken. Arrange the asparagus spears around the chicken and garnish with the caramelized banana and a dollop of the garlic purée. Finish the plate with some of the pickled apple, additional basil and cilantro, and a sprinkle of coarse salt, as desired.

James' Thai-Jewish Chicken

Jewish and Thai are two cuisines I never imagined putting together before Michael and I got together in the ICE kitchens with Chef Watson and *Food & Wine* magazine. As we developed our own takes on the same dish, I did my best to fuse the two cuisines in a single plate. "Tater tots" are just a fancy take on latkes, while Thai flavors show up in the form of curry, basil, and coconut. One ingredient I would not have reached for in this type of dish was the banana, but its sweetness and texture proved the perfect foil for the intensity of the red curry paste.

CHEF WATSON SAYS

SURPRISE   PLEASANTNESS   SYNERGY

Pro Notes and Tips

- Using a chamber vacuum (aka sous vide) allows the pickling liquid to be instantly infused into the apple. If you do not have access to this type of equipment, combine the apples and pickling liquid in a zip-top bag, press out all of the air, and seal. Refrigerate the apples for a minimum of 4 hours before serving. Apples may be made up to 5 days in advance.

THAI GRILLED CHICKEN

    4   boneless, skinless chicken thighs
        kosher salt, to taste
        black pepper, to taste
    ¼   cup (60 grams) coconut milk
    2   teaspoons (12 grams) red curry paste

1. Season the chicken with salt and pepper. Whisk together the coconut milk and curry paste. Rub on the chicken to coat all sides. Refrigerate 2 hours or overnight.

2. Wipe any excess marinade from the chicken. Place the chicken on a hot, oiled grill and cook 6 minutes on the first side, rotating the chicken 90° once during the cooking to achieve hatched grill marks. Flip the chicken and cook an additional 6 minutes, rotating 90° again once. Remove and place on a rack to rest.

BROWN RICE PUFFS

    9   cups (2,000 grams) water
    2   tablespoons (30 grams) kosher salt, plus more
        to taste
    ¼   cup (50 grams) brown sushi rice

1. Combine the water and salt in a pot and bring to a rapid boil. Add the rice and cook until very tender (overcooked). Drain the rice from the pot and spread into a thin layer on a sheet pan. Cool to room temperature, then refrigerate, uncovered, to dry overnight.

2. When the rice is cooled and dried, heat a pot of oil to 400°F (205°C), break the rice into small pieces, and fry until puffed and crisp. Drain on paper towels and season with salt.

TATER TOTS

¼ cup (35 grams) yellow onion, grated
1 tablespoon (10 grams) garlic, minced
2 Idaho potatoes, grated
2 teaspoons (4 grams) kosher salt, plus more as needed
1 cup (225 grams) water
1 teaspoon (4 grams) agar
  oil, as needed

1. Combine the onion, garlic, potato, and salt in a medium-size bowl. Mix well and set aside to soften, 5 to 10 minutes. Squeeze as much liquid as possible from the potato mixture, then break apart the tight ball and return to the bowl.

2. Whisk the water and agar together in a small saucepot. Stir constantly over medium heat until the mixture thickens and begins to bubble. Pour immediately over the potato mixture and mix well to distribute. Divide the mixture into 4 equal portions and roll in plastic wrap to form a tight cylinder shape. Refrigerate to set.

3. To serve, unwrap the potatoes and slice into 1 to 1½-inch pieces. Deep-fry at 350°F (175°C) until golden brown. Drain on paper towels and sprinkle with salt.

BASIL PICKLED APPLE

1 Granny Smith apple
8 fresh basil leaves
½ cup (115 grams) rice wine vinegar
1 teaspoon (4 grams) salt
1 teaspoon (5 grams) sugar

1. Peel the apple and scoop out pieces with a parisienne scoop. Place the pieces into a vacuum bag along with the basil. Whisk together the vinegar, salt, and sugar until dissolved. Add the liquid to the bag with the apples and vacuum seal. Refrigerate until ready to use.

COCONUT FLUID GEL

   1   tablespoon (15 grams) canola oil
   1   cup (120 grams) onion, thinly sliced
   1   teaspoon (6 grams) red curry paste
   1   cup (100 grams) asparagus tips
   3   sprigs basil
   1   vanilla bean, split
   1   tablespoon (6 grams) black peppercorns
 16   fluid ounces (500 grams) vegetable stock
   1   tablespoon (6 grams) agar
13½   fluid-ounce can (400 grams) coconut milk

1. Heat the oil in a medium-size saucepot. Briefly sweat the onions and add the curry paste, asparagus ends, basil, vanilla, pepper, coconut, and stock. Bring the mixture to a simmer and adjust the heat to maintain the simmer—do not let it boil. Cook until reduced by half.

2. Strain the broth into a clean pot. Whisk in the agar and coconut milk. Return the mixture to a simmer, then pour into a pan to cool. When the mixture is firmly set (about 1 hour) break into pieces and transfer to a blender. Process until smooth.

CURRY BROTH

   1   tablespoon (15 grams) canola oil
   1   cup (120 grams) onion, thinly sliced
   1   tablespoon (20 grams) red curry paste
   1   cup (100 grams) asparagus tips
   3   sprigs basil
   1   vanilla bean, split
   2   tablespoons (16 grams) cracked black peppercorns
  ¼   cup (30 grams) coconut, grated
 16   fluid ounces (500 grams) vegetable stock
   2   teaspoon (9 grams) soy lecithin

1. Heat the oil in a medium-size saucepot. Briefly sweat the onions and add the curry paste, asparagus ends, basil, vanilla, pepper, coconut, and stock. Bring the mixture to a simmer and adjust the heat to maintain the simmer—do not let it boil. Cook gently for 45 minutes. Strain the broth and reserve for plating.

2. When ready to serve, heat the broth on the stove top. Add the soy lecithin, remove from the heat, and whip with a hand blender to froth.

CURRIED BANANA GELÉE

   1   green (under-ripe) banana (about 100 grams), split lengthwise
  ¼   cup (60 grams) rice vinegar
   1   tablespoon (20 grams) red curry paste
0.35 gram xanthan gum

1. Combine all of the ingredients in a blender and process until smooth.

TO SERVE

   8   spears asparagus, grilled
        micro cilantro

1. To plate, cut the asparagus on a sharp bias to 2-inch pieces. Cut the grilled chicken into 1-inch square pieces.

2. Place a few pieces of chicken on the plate in a curved line. Place a few dots of the curried banana around the chicken and top each dot with a tater tot. Arrange the asparagus and apples around the chicken. Finish with the micro greens and puffed rice.

Thai-Vietnamese Poutine

Adapting a traditional Canadian dish to the flavors of hot climates was a bit of a challenge. I turned to fresh, cool ingredients to lighten the typical heaviness of a poutine. I was also given sulguni, a briny, salty cheese from Georgia (the country) in the output, which seemed a bit out of left field, as Thailand and Vietnam are traditionally not known for dairy products. But the flavor and mozzarella-like consistency paired perfectly with the tangy spiciness of the gravy, which features tamarind.

—SABRINA SEXTON

CHEF WATSON SAYS

SURPRISE   PLEASANTNESS   SYNERGY

Pro Notes and Tips

- If you can't find sulguni, try feta or mozzarella tossed in vinegar to acquire the tanginess. The gravy could easily be made ahead of time and then warmed up, but don't toss the salad until just before serving.

- For a more elegant sauce and to add extra flavor, you can purée additional cilantro into the sauce, which will give it a smooth texture and bright green color.

4 pounds russet potatoes, peeled
¼ cup (60 grams) lard, plus more for frying
2 tablespoons (36 grams) green curry paste
1 teaspoon (3 grams) licorice
¼ cup (30 grams) flour
4 cups (1,000 grams) chicken stock
1 tablespoon (20 grams) tamarind
1 tablespoon (20 grams) maple syrup
1-2 teaspoons (5 to 10 grams) white vinegar
2 avocados, pitted, peeled, and chopped
1 cup (80 grams) bean sprouts, blanched briefly
1 pear, halved, cored, and julienned
½ cup (45 grams) pickled cucumber
¼ teaspoon (1 gram) dried bird's eye chili
1 tablespoon (15 grams) lime or lemon juice
2 tablespoons (30 grams) olive oil
2 cups (325 grams) sulguni cheese
1-2 tablespoons (10 to 20 grams) cilantro, for garnish
salt and pepper, to taste

1. Cut potatoes into ¼- by ¼-inch strips . Reserve in cold water until ready to fry.

2. Heat the lard in a 2 quart saucepot over medium heat. Add the green curry paste and licorice, cooking briefly until the aromatics are fragrant. Add the flour and continue to stir until the flour begins to toast and develop color (about 5 minutes).

3. Slowly add the stock, stirring with a whisk to avoid lumps. Add the tamarind, maple syrup, and vinegar. Season with salt and pepper. Bring the mixture to a boil and simmer for 5 to 6 minutes (the sauce should thicken). Set aside and keep warm.

4. In a small bowl, combine the avocado, bean sprouts, pear, pickled cucumber, chili, lime juice, and olive oil. Season with salt and pepper, and gently toss. Set aside.

5. Heat the lard to 300°F (150°C) for frying. Remove the potatoes from the oil and dry well with paper towels. Blanch the potatoes for 3 to 4 minutes in oil (until the potatoes are tender, but not brown). Drain on paper towels or a rack.

6. Raise the temperature of the lard to 375 (190°C). Fry the potatoes until golden brown (2 to 3 minutes). Drain and sprinkle with salt.

7. Divide the fries among plates. Pour the sauce over each serving and top with the cheese. Spoon a small amount of the avocado salad over the poutine. Garnish with cilantro and serve immediately.

Sri Lankan-Jamaican Poutine

The most surprising element of this output was the inclusion of whitebait and beef, as "surf and turf" dishes are not typical of either Sri Lankan or Jamaican cultures. The use of beef over the more common goat or chicken is also an interesting element, as is the use of potatoes, which are not indigenous to either country.

—MICHAEL GARRETT

CHEF WATSON SAYS

SURPRISE   PLEASANTNESS   SYNERGY

Pro Notes and Tips

- Whitebait are immature small fish or minnows. If you can't find them, you can substitute sardines or anchovies (fresh, unsalted, and unfermented).

- To prepare the potatoes, cure them in sugar, salt, and baking soda. This boosts the Maillard reaction in the potatoes, producing the perfect golden brown color.

BEEF STEW CURRY SAUCE
- 1 pound beef stew meat
- ¼ cup (56 grams) coconut oil
- 1 small onion, thinly sliced
- 1 Scotch bonnet, thinly sliced
- 1 stalk curry leaf
- 1 tablespoon (15 grams) asafetida
- 3 tablespoons (44 grams) garam masala
- 2 quarts (1,893 grams) fish stock
- 2 cans coconut milk

1. Brown the beef in a cassoulet or Dutch oven in coconut oil and set aside. Add the onion, Scotch bonnet, and curry leaf, and fry until brown.

2. Return the beef to the cassoulet and add the remaining spices and coconut milk. Stew beef until tender.

JERK WHITEBAIT
- 4 ounces whitebait
- 1 teaspoon (5 grams) allspice
- 2 teaspoons (10 grams) smoked paprika
- 1 tablespoon (15 grams) dried thyme
- 1 teaspoon (5 grams) garlic powder
- 1 teaspoon (5 grams) onion powder
- 1 tablespoon (15 grams) chili powder
- 1 cup (237 grams) cornstarch
  vegetable oil, as needed

1. Preheat oil to 340°F (171°C).

2. Toss the whitebait in the spices and cornstarch, and fry.

SORREL MILK CURD
- 2 cups (473 grams) milk
- 1 bunch green sorrel leaves
- ½ cup (118 grams) yogurt
- 2 tablespoons (30 grams) vinegar
  salt, to taste

1. Blend the milk, yogurt, and chiffonade of sorrel leaves. Add the salt and vinegar.

2. Warm the infused milk to 180°F (82°C) until it curdles.

3. Strain the curd through a cheesecloth, discarding the whey. Press the curd into a block and refrigerate.

4. Remove the infused curd and slice for use.

TO SERVE

4   russet potatoes, cut into large batons
    vegetable oil, as needed
    salt and pepper to taste

1. Heat the lard to 325°F (163°C) for frying. Remove the potatoes from the oil and dry well with paper towels. Blanch the potatoes for 3 to 4 minutes in oil (until the potatoes are tender, but not brown). Drain on paper towels or a rack.

2. Raise the temperature of the lard to 375°F (190°C). Fry the potatoes until golden brown (2 to 3 minutes). Drain and sprinkle with salt.

3. Top with the curry sauce and fried whitebait, then finish with the sorrel milk curd.

Pumpkin Brioche with Dates and Mâche Salad

When first served at Berlin's Falling Walls conference, this appetizer course was a pumpkin muffin whose components I have adapted into a yeasted brioche. This recipe serves as a great example of how an ingredient like pumpkin—common in both sweet and savory dishes—can help to bridge the gaps between other ingredients. I find the juxtaposition of the sweet dates and the salty cured pork particularly interesting.

—MICHAEL LAISKONIS

CHEF WATSON SAYS

SURPRISE   PLEASANTNESS   SYNERGY

Pro Notes and Tips

- Yeasted doughs like this brioche get much of their flavor from the slow fermentation process that begins with the pre-ferment: allowing a portion of the flour, water, and yeast to develop ahead of the final dough assembly.

- When adding the butter, it should be neither too cold nor too warm. A cool temperature and slightly pliable consistency can be achieved by removing the butter from the refrigerator about 30 minutes before the final mixing of the brioche.

PUMPKIN BRIOCHE

Pre-Ferment

- 1 cup plus 2 tablespoons (150 grams) all purpose flour
- ¼ cup plus 2 tablespoons (95 grams) whole milk
- ⅛ teaspoon (0.2 gram) instant dry yeast

1. Place the flour, milk, and yeast into a medium-size mixing bowl and stir until combined. Wrap the bowl with plastic film and allow to stand at room temperature for 8 to 12 hours (alternatively, allow to stand at room temperature for 4 hours, then move to the refrigerator for up 12 hours).

Dough

- 1 tablespoon (15 grams) whole milk, slightly warmed
- 1 egg (about 50 grams), room temperature
- ⅓ cup (190 grams) pumpkin, puréed, and room temperature
- 1 teaspoon (20 grams) honey
- 1¾ cup (250 grams) bread flour
- 2½ tablespoons (25 grams) corn meal
- 2 teaspoons (3 grams) instant dry yeast
- 1 teaspoon (5 grams) fine sea salt
- 2 tablespoons (30 grams) granulated sugar
- 2 teaspoons (2 grams) thyme leaves, chopped
- ¼ cup plus 2 tablespoons (90 grams) unsalted butter, room temperature, plus more as needed
  - egg wash, as needed
  - coarse "pretzel" salt, as needed

1. Place the milk, egg, pumpkin, and honey into the bowl of an electric stand mixer fitted with a paddle attachment. Begin mixing and add the remaining dry ingredients and the thyme. Continue to mix on low to medium speed until the dough has formed a cohesive mass. Add the pre-fermented dough and continue, mixing until combined.

2. With the mixer running, begin adding the butter in small amounts. Once the butter has been incorporated, continue mixing on medium speed for an additional 4 minutes or until the dough is stiff and smooth. It may be necessary to stop the mixer occasionally to scrape down the paddle and the sides of the bowl.

 SERVES 6

 1 TO 1½ HOURS, PLUS DOUGH FERMENTATION AND RESTING

 CREATED BY SARAH WIENER REFINED BY MICHAEL LAISKONIS

3. Form the dough into a ball, wrap in plastic film, and ferment at room temperature for 1 hour.

4. Punch down the dough and portion into 2 pieces (400 grams each). Flatten each portion, fold in on itself twice, and roll into an oblong shape (similar to an American football). Place into prepared loaf pans 7- by 4-inches (20- by 10-centimeters), cover with plastic film, and proof for 60 to 90 minutes at room temperature, or until the brioche has nearly doubled in size.

5. Unwrap the loaves and lightly brush with the egg wash. Sprinkle some of the coarse salt over the top of each loaf. Bake in an oven preheated to 320°F (160°C) for 20 to 25 minutes (until golden brown). Remove from the oven and cool before removing from the loaf pans.

POACHED DATES
 1 cup (120 grams) whole dates, pitted
    warm water, as needed for soaking
    juice and zest of 1 lemon
 ¼ cup (60 grams) water
 3 tablespoons (40 grams) granulated sugar

1. Place the dates in a small bowl, cover with warm water, and allow to stand for 10 minutes. Drain dates and carefully remove as much of the loosened skin as possible.

2. Meanwhile, combine the lemon juice and zest with the remaining water and sugar in a small saucepan. Bring to a boil.

3. Add the peeled dates to the lemon syrup and gently simmer on low heat for 5 to 10 minutes. Remove from heat and cool the dates in the syrup. Before serving, drain the dates and discard the syrup.

ORANGE-BALSAMIC VINAIGRETTE
 2 tablespoons (30 grams) orange juice
 2 teaspoons (10 grams) white balsamic vinegar
 1 teaspoon (4 grams) dry mustard powder
 ½ cup (100 grams) olive oil
    fine sea salt, as needed
    cracked black pepper, as needed

1. Combine the orange juice, balsamic, and mustard powder, and whisk together. Slowly drizzle in the olive oil while continuing to whisk.

2. Adjust the acidity with more vinegar if necessary and season with salt and black pepper.

TO SERVE
    2 to 3 small bunches mâche
 3 ounces (85 grams) slab bacon, cut into small cubes, and rendered

1. Wash and spin dry mâche. In a medium-size bowl, combine greens with some of the vinaigrette and toss to coat.

2. Slice the cooled pumpkin brioche as desired and arrange on each plate. Place a portion of the greens alongside the brioche, followed by 3 of the poached dates and a few pieces of bacon.

Italian Chocolate Bread

Chocolate, the star of this dessert, presents endless opportunity in terms of flavor pairing, and it can be expressed in different textures and temperatures, enhanced by a supporting cast of olive oil, pine nuts, dried cherries, and spices. The chocolate bread can be served warm to contrast with the chocolate ice cream, and the unexpected addition of potato chips add a surprising, salty crunch.

—MICHAEL LAISKONIS

CHEF WATSON SAYS

SURPRISE PLEASANTNESS SYNERGY

Pro Notes and Tips

- The zuppa inglese is essentially a custard sauce, similar to what the French would call crème anglaise.

- The final stage of cooking the cream requires a low temperature and constant stirring, as it can easily scorch or curdle.

- This dessert could be refined even further and prepared as a bread pudding: diced bread, pine nuts, and cherries combined with the uncooked zuppa inglese ingredients and baked in a ramekin or glass baking dish.

CHOCOLATE BREAD

¼ cup (60 grams) water
1½ teaspoons (6 grams) instant dry yeast
4 tablespoons (30 grams) Dutch-process cocoa powder
½ teaspoon (3 grams) fine sea salt
3 tablespoons (35 grams) granulated sugar
1¾ cup (250 grams) bread flour
2 large eggs (about 100 grams)
½ cup plus 1 tablespoon (135 grams) unsalted butter, softened
1½ ounces (45 grams) quality dark chocolate, chopped
½ cup (60 grams) dried cherries
¼ cup (50 grams) pine nuts, lightly toasted

1. Place water into the bowl of an electric stand mixer, followed by yeast, cocoa powder, salt, sugar, flour, and eggs.

2. Mix on low speed for 3 minutes to thoroughly combine the ingredients with the paddle or dough hook attachment. Increase the speed to medium and continue mixing for an additional for 3 minutes.

3. Continue mixing and slowly add the butter in small pieces, allowing for each piece to incorporate before adding the next.

4. Continue mixing for 3 to 5 minutes until smooth and shiny. Add the chopped chocolate, the dried cherries, and the pine nuts, and mix just until incorporated.

5. Scrape into bowl, form dough into a ball, and cover with plastic film. Ferment at room temperature for 1 hour.

6. Punch down the dough and divide into 2 pieces (350 grams each). Flatten each portion, fold it in on itself twice, and roll into an oblong shape (similar to an American football). Place into prepared loaf pans measuring 7- by 4-inches (20- by 10-centimeters), cover with plastic film, and proof for 60 to 90 minutes at room temperature, or until the brioche has nearly doubled in size.

7. Unwrap loaves and bake in an oven preheated to 320°F (160°C) for 20 to 25 minutes or until golden brown. Remove from oven and cool before removing from loaf pans.

 SERVES 6 TO 8

 60 TO 90 MINUTES, PLUS DOUGH FERMENTATION AND RESTING

 CREATED BY FLORIAN PINEL
REFINED BY MICHAEL LAISKONIS

CHOCOLATE ICE CREAM

2 tablespoons (15 grams) nonfat dry milk powder
½ cup (100 grams) granulated sugar
3¾ cup (825 grams) whole milk
2 tablespoons (25 grams) honey
8 ounces (240 grams) quality dark chocolate, chopped

1. Combine the dry milk and sugar. Place the milk in a heavy saucepan, whisk in the honey and dry milk mixture, and bring to a boil over medium heat. Remove from heat.

2. Meanwhile, place the chopped chocolate into a large mixing bowl. Gradually incorporate the hot milk into the chocolate. Mix well with an immersion blender. Chill in an ice water bath. Allow mixture to mature in the refrigerator for at least 12 hours.

3. Process mixture in an ice cream machine according to the manufacturer's instructions. Store the finished ice cream in the freezer.

SPICED ZUPPA INGLESE

½ cup (120 grams) heavy cream
1 cup (225 grams) whole milk
1 tablespoon (15 grams) dark rum
½ vanilla bean, split, and scraped
¼ teaspoon (0.5 gram) ground cinnamon
¼ teaspoon (0.5 gram) grated nutmeg
2 tablespoons (50 grams) honey
4 egg yolks (about 80 grams)

1. In a heavy saucepan, combine the cream, milk, rum, vanilla, cinnamon, and nutmeg. Bring to a boil over medium heat. Remove from the heat.

2. Meanwhile, combine the honey and egg yolks in a medium-size bowl and whisk to combine. Gradually temper the hot cream mixture into the egg yolks, whisking constantly. Return to the saucepan.

3. Continue to cook on low heat, stirring continuously until the mixture reaches 185°F (85°C). Remove from heat and strain through a fine mesh sieve. Chill in an ice water bath and refrigerate.

FINGERLING POTATO CHIPS

2 fingerling potatoes, sliced paper thin
olive oil, as needed
fine sea salt, to taste

1. Rinse the potato slices in cold water and thoroughly pat dry on paper towels.

2. Fill a heavy saucepan with oil, no more than halfway, and heat the oil to 350°F (175°C).

3. In small batches, carefully add the potato slices to the oil, and fry until light golden brown (30 to 60 seconds). Remove from the oil, drain on paper towels, and lightly season with salt.

TO SERVE

confectioners sugar, as needed for dusting
Dutch-process cocoa powder, as needed for dusting

1. Slice the chocolate bread as desired and gently warm the slices in a toaster or an oven. Place each slice in a bowl and dust with confectioners sugar and a small amount of cocoa powder. Top with a scoop of the chocolate ice cream and potato chips, followed by a drizzle of the zuppa inglese.

Blue Caribbean Hurricane

Given IBM's fondness for the color blue, it was only a matter of time before someone asked Chef Watson to create a blue cocktail. Blue is the one color that doesn't have much of a natural place in food, but I was up for the challenge. Instead of going with the obvious Blue Curaçao—whose only noteworthy quality is its color—I came up with a recipe using blueberries, thinking that the mixture might turn blue if I added baking soda (the anthocyanin in blueberries may appear red, purple, or blue depending on the pH). In the end, however, practicality won out. Blue Curaçao hurricane, anyone?

—FLORIAN PINEL

Pro Notes and Tips

- Run warm water over the can of coconut cream before using it to ensure it has liquified.

- For large parties, mix all of the ingredients, except for the Sprite, in a punch bowl.

PREPARATION

1½	ounces coconut cream
3	ounces Bacardi or other white rum
3	ounces banana juice
4	ounces pineapple juice
½	ounce lime juice
½	ounce blue curaçao
5	ounces Sprite

1. In a shaker, mix the coconut cream, rum, banana juice, pineapple juice, lime juice, and Blue Curaçao in a shaker.

2. Pour into 5-ounce cocktail or hurricane glasses and top with Sprite (roughly a 2:1 punch mix to Sprite ratio).

French Champagne Punch

This punch, based on autumnal flavors, offers a great deal of surprise with only a few ingredients. Its elegance and slightly more advanced preparation make it the exact opposite of the Blue Curaçao hurricane. Replacing the Champagne with another dry white sparkling wine can achieve very similar results.

—FLORIAN PINEL

CHEF WATSON SAYS

SURPRISE

PLEASANTNESS

SYNERGY

Pro Notes and Tips

- To make this drink in a punch bowl, multiply the ingredient quantities by the number of guests you're serving and mix everything, except the Champagne, in advance.

- Cover and refrigerate, then add the Champagne and ice just before service.

 ⅔ ounce orange juice
 ⅔ ounce cognac
     dash lemon juice
1⅔ ounces Champagne
 2 raspberries (about 8 grams)
 1 cube (about 4 grams) McIntosh apple

APPLE-HONEY-GINGER MIXTURE

12 ounces apple juice
3⅕ ounces clover honey
 ¼ teaspoon (0.7 gram) ground ginger

1. Pour half of the apple juice into a saucepan and bring to a simmer over medium heat.

2. Add honey and ground ginger. Stir until well-mixed.

3. Transfer to a plastic container, add the rest of the apple juice. Let cool, then refrigerate.

1. For 1 serving, combine 2 ounces of the apple-ginger mixture, plus orange juice, cognac, and lemon juice, and stir.

2. Pour mixture into a 7-ounce glass and top with champagne.

3. Garnish the glass with 2 raspberries and 1 cube of apple on a bamboo skewer.

Party Bourbon Punch

What does the Watson team do when they want to throw a party? They make cocktails with Chef Watson, of course! We created this punch for the release of the *Bon Appétit* beta app, happily playing mixologists and guinea pigs until the bourbon (almost) ran out. Most people don't imagine pairing bourbon and pineapple, in part because they hail from different climates. Yet, it works.

—FLORIAN PINEL

CHEF WATSON SAYS

SURPRISE

PLEASANTNESS

SYNERGY

Pro Notes and Tips

- For an even brighter flavor, use freshly squeezed orange and lime juices (instead of bottled juices).

PREPARATION:

- 3 ounces bourbon
- 3 ounces pineapple juice
- 2 ounces orange juice
  splash lime juice
- 3 ounces hard cider
- 2 slices orange
- 2 slices peach

1. Fill a shaker with ice. Add the bourbon, pineapple juice, orange juice, and lime juice, then shake.

2. Pour the cocktail into glasses. Top with the hard cider and stir gently. Garnish with the orange and peach slices.

 SERVES 2

2 MINUTES

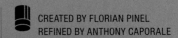
CREATED BY FLORIAN PINEL
REFINED BY ANTHONY CAPORALE

Japanese Wasabi Cocktail

This unique elixir combines the classic Eastern flavors of sake and wasabi, brightened with the juice of fresh lime. Utterly Japanese in its simplicity, the drink is both casual and elegant, making it perfect for any event, from a summer afternoon cookout to a formal evening dinner party.

CHEF WATSON SAYS

SURPRISE   PLEASANTNESS   SYNERGY

Pro Notes and Tips

- The lime juice makes or breaks this drink, so be sure to use only fresh, ripe limes that were purchased no more than one day earlier.

- Roll the lime between your palm and a cutting board before juicing to soften the pulp and increase yield.

WASABI WATER
- 1   bar spoon wasabi powder
- 2   ounces water

1. In a mixing glass, mix the wasabi powder and water, stirring well to dissolve.

TO SERVE
- 2   ounces sake
  - juice of ½ lime, plus lime hull
- ½   ounce wasabi water
- 3   sprigs thyme

1. In a mixing tin half-filled with ice, add the sake, lime juice and hull, wasabi water, and 2 sprigs of thyme.

2. Shake until the tin is frosted.

3. Strain into a Collins glass over fresh ice and garnish with a sprig of fresh thyme.

5 Home Cooking With Watson

When the editors of *Bon Appétit* heard about cognitive cooking, they were curious to see what would happen if a leading food magazine tapped into Watson's expertise. So they contacted IBM's Steve Abrams, who leads Watson's consumer-facing initiatives, and within a few weeks, a collaboration was born.

The challenge for *Bon Appétit* and IBM was to come up with innovative dishes that would still fit the magazine's audience: home cooks and consumers

with a passion for food. Up until that point, Chef Watson had been searching for ingredients and combinations in the endless Wikia database, a collection in which almost anything goes. So for this collaboration, we limited Watson's explorations to the 9,000 or so recipes in *Bon Appétit*'s recipe database.

Soon Watson was churning out ingredient lists drawn from this narrower and more select archive. What's more, the computer studied not only the ingredients in the *Bon Appétit*

recipes, but also the instructions and proportions. With the launch of the Chef Watson beta app, a select group of *Bon Appétit* customers were invited to create recipes with Watson—the first time the system was used by home cooks. This venture thus represented a vital step in the evolution of cognitive cooking.

True to form, Watson's initial recipes packed plenty of surprising blends of cultures and flavors. Gazpacho with ginger would surprise foodies from Seville to Bangalore. But the chefs at *Bon Appétit* were able to fit these exciting new dishes within the publication's style and traditions, which means that these recipes, like most that appear in the magazine, are tailored to the avid home cook and a bit more simple to prepare than others in the Chef Watson oeuvre.

Spicy Tomato Gazpacho with Ginger

Blending in the avocado, as Watson originally intended, would have made a muddy brown gazpacho, so we took the avocado out of the blender and garnished the soup with it instead.

SURPRISE   PLEASANTNESS   SYNERGY

Pro Notes and Tips

• Carefully removing the seeds and interior ribs of the jalapeño will help regulate its heat. A touch of smoky chipotle might also accent the dish.

CROUTONS

1 thick slice of country bread, torn into bite-sized pieces
2 tablespoons extra virgin olive oil
  kosher salt, to taste
  freshly ground black pepper, to taste

1. Preheat an oven to 425°F (218°C). Toss the bread with olive oil and salt, and transfer to a baking sheet. Bake for 3 to 4 minutes. Toss the croutons, and bake an additional 3 to 4 minutes until golden in color.

GAZPACHO

1 tablespoon extra virgin olive oil
1 cup leeks (white part only), rinsed, and finely chopped
  kosher salt, to taste
2 tablespoons dry sherry
1 large beefsteak tomato, cored, and chopped
4 teaspoons fresh ginger, minced
12 ounces cherry tomatoes
1 cucumber, peeled, seeded, and chopped
1 jalapeño, seeded, and chopped
4 teaspoons white balsamic vinegar
½ cup water
  freshly ground black pepper, to taste

1. Heat the olive oil in a saucepan over medium high heat. Add the leeks and season with salt. Cook, stirring often, until softened (5 to 7 minutes). Add the sherry and cook until almost completely reduced. Add the beefsteak tomato and ginger. Cook, stirring until the tomato just begins to release its juices (about 2 minutes). Remove from heat and allow to cool.

2. Combine the leek mixture with the cherry tomatoes, cucumber, jalapeño, balsamic vinegar, and water in a blender, and purée until very smooth (about 2 minutes). Season with salt and pepper, and thin with water as necessary for desired consistency.

TO SERVE

  1 avocado, pitted, chopped
  1 tablespoon dill, finely chopped
     extra virgin olive oil, as needed

1. Divide the gazpacho among serving bowls and top with the croutons, chopped avocado, dill, and a drizzle of olive oil.

Roasted Tomato and Mozzarella Tart

Ultimately, we omitted the flour and cornmeal Watson suggested from the tart filling, as well as the smoked paprika, which was really overwhelming. But what a stunner! Think of this recipe as pizza's fancy cousin who spent a semester abroad in Paris. It's an elegant tart that presents beautifully, yet has all the flavors of an old favorite. The baked tart is equally delicious served hot or cold.

CHEF WATSON SAYS

SURPRISE   PLEASANTNESS   SYNERGY

Pro Notes and Tips

• Roast the tomatoes before adding them to the filling to help concentrate flavor and eliminate excess moisture, which would result in a runny filling.

• When checking for doneness, remove the tart from the oven when the center is still a little soft, as the filling will continue to cook and set.

• Freezing the puff pastry helps to hold its shape when baking. It is well worth waiting the half hour.

1   14-ounce sheet puff pastry, thawed according to package directions
12 ounces cherry tomatoes, halved
3   plum tomatoes, cored, and quartered
4   sage leaves
3   sprigs oregano
1   sprig rosemary
2   tablespoons olive oil
    kosher salt
    freshly ground pepper
2   eggs
¼   cup whole milk
¼   cup sour cream
¼   teaspoon cayenne pepper
8   ounces mozzarella, torn into bite-sized pieces

1. Preheat oven to 425°F. On a lightly floured surface, roll the puff pastry out to a 12-inch circle. Carefully transfer to a 10-inch tart pan, leaving a 1-inch overhang. Fold the overhang in and press to seal. Prick bottom of the pastry all over with a fork. Freeze 30 minutes.

2. Meanwhile, toss the cherry tomatoes, plum tomatoes, and herbs with olive oil, and season with salt and pepper. Roast until tomatoes collapse and begin to blister (25 to 30 minutes). Set aside to cool.

3. Place the tart shell on a rimmed baking sheet. Cover the pastry with parchment or foil, leaving a 2-inch overhang, and fill with pie weights or dried beans. Bake until edges are golden brown (20 to 25 minutes). Remove pie weights and parchment, and continue to bake until bottom is golden brown (10 to 15 minutes).

4. Beat together the eggs, milk, sour cream, and cayenne, and season with salt and pepper. Arrange the tomatoes, herbs, and mozzarella inside the tart shell and top with the egg mixture.

5. Bake until the cheese is melted and egg is set (30 to 35 minutes). Cool before serving.

Fennel-Spiced Ribs with Tangy Apple-Mustard Barbecue Sauce

Slow cooking ribs in the oven, then finishing them on the grill, is the perfect way to get the meat tender and juicy, with a gentle smoky flavor. Here, the surprise really comes in the sauce. Oyster sauce provides depth and umami you are unlikely to find in a standard barbeque sauce, while Chinese mustard brings heat. Rounded out with more familiar flavors like apple juice and bourbon, the sauce is truly a East meets West mash-up.

CHEF WATSON SAYS

SURPRISE   PLEASANTNESS   SYNERGY

Pro Notes and Tips

- The ribs can be baked up to 3 days ahead and wrapped tightly in foil or plastic. The flavor will intensify and the cold ribs will hold together better when reheated. (Reserve juices and chill separately after baking.)

- Bring ribs back to room temperature before grilling.

- If you have trouble locating Chinese hot mustard, use Creole or spicy brown mustard.

RIBS

- 1 tablespoon coriander seeds
- 2 tablespoons fennel seeds
- 2 tablespoons kosher salt
- 1 tablespoon fresh oregano, chopped
- 1 tablespoon fresh rosemary, chopped
- 1 tablespoon sugar
- 2 teaspoons chili powder
- 2 teaspoons smoked paprika
- 2 racks baby back pork ribs (about 6 pounds)

1. Preheat the oven to 350°F. Toast the coriander and fennel seeds in a dry small skillet over medium heat, tossing until fragrant (about 3 minutes). Let cool, then finely chop with a knife or coarsely grind in a spice mill. Transfer to a small bowl and mix with the salt, oregano, rosemary, sugar, chili powder, and paprika.

2. Place each rack of ribs on double-layered sheets of foil. Sprinkle the spice mixture all over the ribs. Wrap and place on a rimmed baking sheet. Bake the ribs until very tender, but not until the meat is falling from the bone (about 2 hours).

3. Carefully unwrap the ribs (there will be a lot of steam) and transfer to a platter. Let cool. Pour any cooking juices from the foil into a heatproof measuring cup. Set aside.

SAUCE AND ASSEMBLY

- ¼ cup apple juice
- ¼ cup white wine vinegar
- 3 tablespoons oyster sauce
- 1 tablespoon bourbon
- 1 tablespoon dark brown sugar
- 1 tablespoon olive oil
- 1 tablespoon Dijon mustard
- 1 teaspoon hot Chinese mustard

1. Preheat a grill on high heat. Whisk the apple juice, vinegar, oyster sauce, bourbon, brown sugar, oil, Dijon mustard, and Chinese mustard into reserved rib juices.

2. Grill the ribs, turning and basting with sauce often, until heated through, glazed, and charred in spots (8 to 10 minutes). Transfer to a cutting board, and cut racks between the bones into individual ribs. Transfer to a platter and serve with the remaining sauce alongside.

Scallops with Tomato Relish and Green Tomato Consommé

This is by far the most ambitious Watson collaboration we've seen from the home cooks. While some of the quantities were initially off for 4 servings, this became a beautiful and balanced dish. Bravo!

Pro Notes and Tips

- Don't move scallops once they hit the pan. This will help them develop a deep golden crust.

- Making cilantro oil is a great way to infuse flavor, and the technique can be applied to virtually any soft herb.

- Charring the tomatillos and peppers for the consommé adds a smoky depth of flavor—a wonderful foil to the fresh tomato relish and the rich scallops.

CILANTRO OIL
- 1 cup lightly packed cilantro leaves and tender stems
- ½ cup olive oil

1. Cook cilantro in a small pot of boiling salted water until wilted, about 15 seconds. Transfer to a bowl of ice water to cool, then drain, squeezing out as much water as possible between paper towels.

2. Combine the cilantro and olive oil in a blender and purée until smooth (about 1 minute). Set aside to steep for 1 hour. Strain through a fine mesh sieve lined with cheesecloth.

GREEN TOMATO CONSOMMÉ
- 2 tomatillos
- 1 habañero chile
- 1 jalapeño chile
- 1 poblano chile
- 4 green tomatoes, cored, and chopped
- 2 celery stalks, chopped
- 1 cucumber, peeled, seeded, and chopped
- 1 tablespoon rice vinegar
- 1 tablespoon white balsamic vinegar
  kosher salt, freshly ground pepper

1. Heat a medium cast iron skillet over medium high heat. Add tomatillos, habañero, jalapeño, and poblano, and cook, turning often, until charred on all sides (6 to 8 minutes). Cool, then seed and chop chilies. Place the chilies in a blender with the tomatillos, green tomatoes, celery, cucumber, rice vinegar, and white balsamic vinegar. Purée until smooth and season with salt and pepper.

2. Transfer tomato mixture to a 9- by 13-inch baking dish and freeze until solid, at least 2 hours. Scrape up mixture with a fork and transfer to a fine-mesh sieve. Let melt over sieve until you have about 1 cup liquid. Discard solids.

SCALLOPS AND ASSEMBLY

- 1 heirloom tomato, seeded, and finely chopped
- 1 small shallot, finely chopped
- 1 tablespoon white balsamic vinegar
- 2 teaspoons fresh cilantro, chopped
- 1 teaspoon fresh chives, chopped
  kosher salt
  freshly ground pepper
- 1 tablespoon vegetable oil
- 12 large scallops
  Maldon salt, to taste

1. Combine tomato, shallot, vinegar, cilantro, and chives in a small bowl. Season with salt and pepper.

2. Heat oil in a large skillet over medium high heat. Season the scallops with salt and pepper, and cook until deep golden brown (about 3 minutes per side).

3. Divide tomato relish among plates and top with the scallops. Spoon the consommé around scallops and drizzle with cilantro oil. Season with Maldon salt.

Tamarind Cabbage Slaw with Crispy Onions

Here is proof that fried onions are good on anything—even a slaw. This dish really shines thanks to the brightness of fresh herbs. Fish sauce and tamarind, two ingredients essential to Southeast Asian cuisine, were certainly a surprise when Watson suggested them as part of a Fouth of July picnic spread. Yet, as always, the results are delicious.

CHEF WATSON SAYS

SURPRISE   PLEASANTNESS   SYNERGY

Pro Notes and Tips

- You can make the fried onions in advance. Reserve them on a wire rack and toss with slaw just before serving.

- If you don't have fish sauce, substitute with soy sauce.

- Mix the slaw and dressing well ahead of serving, with the exception of the fried onions. The flavor will improve as it sits.

CRISPY ONIONS

½   medium white onion, thinly sliced
¼   cup buttermilk
¼   cup mayonnaise
    kosher salt, to taste
    freshly ground pepper, to taste
8   cups vegetable oil
1   cup all purpose flour
1   teaspoon chili powder

1. Whisk buttermilk and mayonnaise in a medium bowl. Season with salt and pepper. Add onions and toss to coat. Let sit 15 minutes.

2. Meanwhile, fill a large saucepan with 2 inches of oil. Heat over medium high heat to 375°F.

3. Whisk flour and chili powder in a shallow dish. Season with salt and pepper. Working in batches, remove onion from buttermilk, letting the excess drip back into bowl, toss in seasoned flour, and fry, turning occasionally, until golden brown and crisp (about 4 minutes). Transfer to a wire rack set inside a rimmed baking sheet. Season with salt.

SLAW AND ASSEMBLY

3   tablespoons unseasoned rice vinegar
2   tablespoons olive oil
1   tablespoon fish sauce (such as nam pla or nuoc nam)
1   tablespoon honey
2   teaspoons tamarind concentrate
½   medium head of green cabbage (about 6 cups), thinly sliced
4   scallions, thinly sliced
1   cup fresh basil leaves, torn
1   cup fresh mint leaves, torn
½   cup salted, roasted peanuts, chopped

1. Whisk vinegar, oil, fish sauce, honey, and tamarind in a large bowl. Season with salt and pepper. Add cabbage, scallions, basil, mint, and peanuts, and toss to combine.

2. Serve slaw topped with crispy onions.

Grilled Corn and Nectarine Salad with Toasted Spice Vinaigrette

There are times when the act of simply reading through a recipe makes one hungry, and this vibrant side dish is one of them. The sweet combination of corn and nectarine, unified by the warm spices of cumin and coriander, is an unforgettable pairing.

Pro Notes and Tips

- One ear of corn produces about a ½ cup of kernels.

- This dish evokes the classic grilled corn elote, a favorite among Mexican street foods.

- Substituting lime juice for part or all of the lemon in the vinaigrette will work equally well. You can also replace coriander seeds with leaves of fresh coriander, better known as cilantro.

4 ears corn, husked
1 tablespoon plus ¼ cup olive oil
  kosher salt
¾ teaspoon chili powder
½ teaspoon coriander seeds
½ teaspoon cumin seeds
3 tablespoons fresh lemon juice
½ teaspoon fresh rosemary, chopped
  several dashes of hot sauce
  freshly ground black pepper
2 nectarines or peaches, sliced into ½-inch thick wedges
1 small shallot, thinly sliced
1 cup fresh basil leaves, torn
½ cup crumbled queso panela or Cotija cheese

1. Prepare grill for medium high heat. Brush corn with a total of 1 tablespoon oil. Season with salt and sprinkle with chili powder. Grill, turning occasionally, until tender and lightly charred in spots (6 to 8 minutes). Transfer to a cutting board and let cool, then cut kernels from cobs.

2. Meanwhile, toast coriander and cumin seeds in a dry skillet over medium heat, tossing, until fragrant (about 3 minutes). Let cool, then chop with a knife or coarsely grind in a spice mill. Whisk with lemon juice, rosemary, hot sauce, and remaining ¼ cup oil in a medium bowl. Season with salt and pepper. Add corn kernels, nectarines, shallot, basil, and cheese, and toss to combine.

Blackberry-Cherry Cobbler with Honey Whipped Cream

On the surface, this seasonal summer dessert may seem straightforward, but it is worth noting that Watson brilliantly balanced fruity, spicy, and acidic flavors along with the novel addition of the fragrant herb marjoram.

CHEF WATSON SAYS

SURPRISE   PLEASANTNESS   SYNERGY

Pro Notes and Tips

- Like any biscuit, this one needs a gentle touch. Do not overwork the dough or it will get tough.

- The perfect vehicle for in-season fruit, this cobbler can be made any time of year using frozen cherries and blackberries in either a large format dessert, as pictured, or baked in individual portions.

FILLING

- 2 pounds fresh or frozen blackberries (about 3½ cups)
- 1 pound fresh or frozen sweet cherries (about 2 cups), pitted
- ½ cup sugar
- 3 tablespoons all purpose flour
- 2 tablespoons fresh lemon juice
- 1 tablespoon fresh marjoram, chopped
- 1 teaspoon vanilla extract
- ½ teaspoon ground cinnamon
- ¼ teaspoon kosher salt

1. Heat oven to 350°F. Toss the blackberries, cherries, sugar, flour, lemon juice, marjoram, vanilla, cinnamon, and salt in a large bowl. Transfer to a shallow 3-quart baking dish.

BISCUIT TOPPING AND ASSEMBLY

- 2 cups all purpose flour
- 2 teaspoons baking powder
- 1 teaspoon kosher salt
- 2 tablespoons sugar, divided
- ½ cup (1 stick) chilled unsalted butter, cut into pieces
- ¾ cup buttermilk
- 1 egg, beaten
- ½ cup heavy cream
- ½ cup sour cream
- 1 tablespoon honey
- 1 tablespoon confectioners sugar

1. Pulse the flour, baking powder, salt, and 1 tablespoon sugar in a food processor to combine. Add the butter and pulse until the dough is the texture of coarse meal. Transfer mixture to a large bowl. Using a spoon, mix in the buttermilk, then gently knead a few times until dough comes together. Drop mounds of biscuit over the pie filling, brush with egg, and sprinkle with remaining 1 tablespoon sugar.

2. Place the cobbler on a baking sheet and bake, tenting with foil if the topping becomes too dark before the filling is tender, until the filling is bubbling and the topping is golden brown (35 to 40 minutes). Transfer to a wire rack and let cool slightly.

3. Just before serving, whisk cream, sour cream, honey, and confectioners sugar to soft peaks. Serve cobbler topped with whipped cream mixture.

6 51 Astor Place

It was a whirlwind year that took Chef Watson and team across the globe, from a virtual unknown to a ground-breaking technology. But as summer of 2014 turned to fall, it was time for Watson's homecoming—to a new home in New York City's Astor Place.

There, in the heart of New York's Silicon Alley, IBM opened a stunning new headquarters for its Watson Group, designed by the famed architect Fumihiko Maki. The Watson Group is a business division given the task of commercializing cognitive computing technologies that can learn, answer questions, draw insights from oceans of raw data, and interact with people in ways that seem intuitive and surprising—even human. The new building houses a design studio, a space for imagining new uses for Watson technologies, and a number of interactive labs. The work done there runs the gamut, from developing personalized medicine to designing smarter cities.

Who better to lay out the banquet for the building's grand opening than Chef Watson and the chefs from New York City's Institute of Culinary Education?

For this New York City-themed event, Watson and the ICE chefs came up with sweet and savory new dishes inspired by neighborhoods throughout the Big Apple. The dishes range from Italian Pumpkin Cheesecake, in honor of the legendary Italian dining neighborhood of Arthur Avenue in the Bronx, to Baltic Herring Salad, inspired by the Russian neighborhood of Brighton Beach near Coney Island. With the Astor Place celebration, IBM and ICE took New York's ethnic neighborhoods back to their roots with a cognitive computing twist.

Tanzanian-Lithuanian Bagel

We started our hunt for a breakfast item by plugging in an Eastern European cuisine alongside "bagel." For a challenge, we added "Tanzanian," which is a cuisine most would not associate with bagels, plus one that few chefs know anything about. In the end, these chemical flavor affinities are at some of the highest levels we've seen.

CHEF WATSON SAYS

SURPRISE   PLEASANTNESS   SYNERGY

Pro Notes and Tips

- Though it greatly increases the prep time, commercial smoked chicken breast can be swapped with homemade: Soak the chicken breasts in a cumin- and cayenne-scented brine solution (5% salt by weight of water) for 3 to 4 hours and slowly hot-smoke to an internal temperature of 165°F (74°C) on a charcoal grill.

- The pickled carrots benefit from marinating several hours in the pickling liquid.

PICKLED CARROTS

- 1   medium carrot, peeled, and cut into thin ribbons
- ½   cup (120 grams) water, plus more as needed
- 1   teaspoon (5 grams) fine sea salt
- ⅔   cup (80 grams) cider vinegar
- 1   tablespoon (15 grams) brown sugar
- ½   teaspoon (1 gram) cumin seeds
- ½   teaspoon (1 gram) cayenne pepper

1. Bring a small saucepan of salted water to a boil.

2. Add the sliced carrot and simmer for about 30 seconds. Drain into a colander and rinse under cold water. Drain thoroughly.

3. In the same saucepan, bring the remaining ingredients to a boil. Reduce heat and simmer for 2 minutes.

4. Remove from heat and add the blanched carrot. Allow to cool and reserve under refrigeration.

BLUE CHEESE SPREAD

- ¾   cup (80 grams) blue cheese, crumbled
- 2   tablespoons (30 grams) cream cheese, softened
- 1   tablespoon (15 grams) unsalted butter, softened

1. Combine all of the ingredients in a small bowl and thoroughly mix together until smooth.

TO SERVE

- 4   bagels, split, and toasted
- 8   ounces (240 grams) smoked chicken breast, thinly sliced
     parsley leaves, as needed
     basil leaves, as needed

1. Apply a thin layer of the blue cheese spread onto the bottom half of each bagel and arrange slices of smoked chicken (roughly 2 ounces each) and drained pickled carrot. Finish with fresh parsley and basil; top each with the remaining upper half of each bagel.

Dutch-Brazilian Vanilla Croissant

The spices and a flavorful dried mushroom powder were easy enough to work into the initial dough and glaze, but I struggled with how to introduce mint, worried that it would be easily obscured. In the end, using fresh mint as a final garnish offered the most interesting option. This croissant dough begins with a pre-fermented starter, allowing for greater flavor development.

Pro Notes and Tips

- Proofing at too high of a temperature (above 90°F/32°C) will cause the thin layers of butter to melt and "weep" from the finished croissants, resulting in a dense, tough finished product. It is best to proof at room temperature.

- While the entire process extends over 2 days, the dough (after the final turn) can be frozen for up to 2 weeks, to bake at a later date.

PRE-FERMENTED STARTER

- ½ cup (120 grams) whole milk
- 1 tablespoon (15 grams) light brown sugar
- ¾ cup (130 grams) bread flour
- 1 teaspoon (3 grams) instant dry yeast

1. Combine the ingredients for the pre-ferment and mix to achieve a soft dough. Cover and allow to sit at room temperature for 2 to 3 hours.

DETREMPE

- 1½ cups (130 grams) all purpose flour
- 1½ teaspoons (8 grams) fine sea salt
- scant ¼ teaspoon (0.5 gram) ground cinnamon
- scant ¼ teaspoon (0.5 gram) turmeric powder
- ½ cup plus 1 tablespoon (140 grams) whole milk
- 1 tablespoon (20 grams) sour cream

1. Place the flour, salt, and spices into the bowl of an electric stand mixer and combine well with the paddle attachment. Add the milk and sour cream, followed by the pre-fermented starter. Mix on low speed until the mass comes together.

2. Increase the mixer speed and continue to work the dough until it is strong and elastic, about 4 minutes.

3. Cover and allow the dough to bulk ferment for 1 hour at room temperature. Punch down the dough and roll into a rectangle measuring roughly 12- by 16-inches (30- by 40-centimeters). Transfer the dough sheet to a parchment-lined baking pan and refrigerate for a minimum of 12 hours, or up to 24 hours.

BEURRAGE

- 2 cups (250 grams) unsalted butter, softened
- 1 teaspoon (2 grams) dried porcini mushroom powder
- all purpose flour, as needed for rolling
- egg wash, as needed

1. Combine the softened butter and porcini powder, and mix thoroughly to combine.

2. Spread the butter mixture onto a sheet of parchment paper cut to 8- by 12-inches (20- by 30-centimeters), ensuring an even thickness and a clean, rectangular shape. Wrap and chill.

3. To begin the rolling process, place the chilled dough sheet onto a lightly floured work surface and place the butter rectangle over half of the dough (the rectangle of dough should be roughly twice the size of the butter). Fold the dough over the butter to enclose, and pinch the edges of the dough together.

4. Position the dough so that the shorter end of the rectangle is facing you and roll the dough in one direction to create a longer rectangle, measuring 8- by 24-inches (20- by 60-centimeters) .

5. Brush off any excess flour and fold the rectangle in thirds, as one would fold a letter. This is the first single turn. Place the dough in the refrigerator and allow to rest for 30 minutes before rolling and completing second turn.

6. In the same manner as the first turn, roll the dough to roughly the same dimensions and fold into thirds a second time. Refrigerate and rest an additional 30 minutes.

7. Complete a third and final turn, also with a 30-minute resting period. At this point the dough can remain in the refrigerator for up to 12 hours.

8. When ready to shape the croissants, divide the dough in half and roll each portion to a rectangle measuring roughly 20- by 12-inches (50- by 30-centimeters) wide, and just less than ⅜-inch (1-centimeter) thick. Square the dough and cut in half to create two rectangles measuring 6- by 20-inches (15- by 50-centimeters).

9. Mark 3-inch (7-centimeter) increments along the length of the dough, and cut diagonally along the width to create about 10 to 12 triangles (for larger croissants, simply adjust the measurements to a large triangle).

 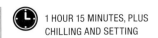

10. Cut a 1-inch (2.5-centimeter) notch at the base of each triangle and pull the corners apart slightly, rolling the triangle from base to tip into croissant form.

11. Transfer the shaped croissant to a parchment-lined sheet pan. Loosely cover with plastic and allow to slowly proof at a warm room temperature for 1 to 2 hours (until nearly doubled in size).

12. When fully proofed, gently brush each croissant with the egg wash and bake in a preheated oven at 350°F (175°C) for 15 to 20 minutes (until a deep golden brown). Remove from the oven and cool.

VANILLA-PORCINI GLAZE

- ½ cup (150 grams) sweetened condensed milk
- ½ teaspoon (2 grams) vanilla extract
- ½ teaspoon (grams) porcini mushroom powder

1. Place all the ingredients in a small bowl and whisk to combine.

TO SERVE

Fresh mint, as needed

1. Arrange the cooled croissants on a parchment-lined sheet pan and apply the glaze by drizzling or brushing over the top. Finish with a few individual mint leaves.

Baltic Herring Salad

I didn't grow up with a taste for herring, but my travels through the Baltics and Scandinavia as an adult quickly made me a convert. The output here demonstrates how the Watson system can support what we consider classic flavor pairings while teaching chefs about a new cuisine. During my research for this dish, I stumbled upon a traditional Russian condiment called ikra, an eastern European version of eggplant "caviar."

CHEF WATSON SAYS

SURPRISE   PLEASANTNESS   SYNERGY

Pro Notes and Tips

- The usual pickled herring will work just fine in this dish, but the seasonal "new catch" Holland herring that arrives in the spring and summer is a special treat. It is only lightly salt cured, preserving the rich flavor and texture of the fish. Alternately, smoked herring also makes for a delicious option.

| SERVES 6   45 TO 50 MINUTES, PLUS ROASTING, COOLING, AND PICKLING   MICHAEL LAISKONIS

PICKLED RED ONION

- 1 small red onion (about 120 grams), peeled, and thinly sliced into rings or julienned
- ½ teaspoon (5 grams) granulated sugar
- ¾ teaspoon (4 grams) fine sea salt
- ¼ cup (60 grams) water
- ½ cup (120 grams) rice vinegar or white wine vinegar
- 1 clove garlic, peeled, halved
- 5 whole black peppercorns
- 1 bay leaf
- 3 small sprigs fresh dill
- ¼ teaspoon (0.5 gram) cayenne pepper

1. To lightly blanch the onion, bring a small saucepan of water to a boil. Remove from heat and add the sliced onions. Allow to stand for a few seconds and drain. Transfer to a bowl of cold water to halt the cooking process and drain again.

2. Place the blanched onion in a small jar or lidded container. Meanwhile, place all of the remaining ingredients in a small saucepan and bring to a simmer, stirring to dissolve the salt and sugar.

3. Remove from heat and add the water–vinegar mixture (along with all of the flavorings) into the container with the onions. Allow to cool at room temperature and then refrigerate for at least 30 minutes (the pickled onions will keep in the refrigerator for up to a week or more).

CURRIED EGGPLANT IKRA

- 1 small eggplant
- 1 tablespoon (15 grams) vegetable or olive oil, divided
- 2 tablespoons (20 grams) onion, finely diced
- 1 small clove garlic, finely chopped
- ½ teaspoon (0.5 gram) madras curry powder
- 1½ tablespoon (20 grams) fresh lemon juice
- 1 tablespoon (2 grams) parsley, finely chopped
  fine sea salt, to taste
  freshly ground black pepper, to taste

1. Using a fork, prick holes in the eggplant at regular intervals and rub roughly half of the oil over the surface. Place on a lined sheet pan and roast in a preheated 350°F (175°C) oven for 30 to 40 minutes, or until the skin has blistered slightly and the flesh of the eggplant is very soft.

2. Remove the eggplant from the oven and cool. Carefully peel the skin and green stem from the eggplant. To reduce bitterness, squeeze and drain excess liquid from the flesh and discard any large pockets of seeds.

3. Meanwhile, heat the remaining oil in a small sauté pan and gently sweat the onion and garlic, along with the curry powder, cooking just until softened and fragrant. Remove from the heat and combine the eggplant, onion mixture, lemon juice, and chopped parsley in the bowl of a food processor. Pulse the machine until a barely smooth purée is formed.

4. Season the mixture with salt and pepper, and adjust the consistency with a bit more oil or lemon juice if desired. Refrigerate until assembly.

CHARRED ONION

- 6 pearl onions
- ½ cup (120 grams) water or chicken stock
- 2 teaspoons (10 grams) unsalted butter
  fine sea salt, to taste

1. Peel each onion and slice in half crosswise. Begin to heat a heavy iron skillet or sauté pan and place each onion half, cut side down, onto the dry pan. Apply moderate pressure, and cook for 2 to 3 minutes over medium heat, allowing the onion to blacken. Remove from the heat and allow the onions to cool.

2. Trim the root or bulb ends from each onion half and place in a saucepan, cut side up, and gently simmer with the water or stock until tender and the liquid has reduced. Glaze onions with a small amount of butter and season with salt. Reserve warm or at room temperature.

LEMON CRÈME FRAÎCHE

- ½ cup (100 grams) crème fraîche
  juice and grated zest of ½ lemon (15 grams of juice)
  freshly ground black pepper, to taste

1. Whisk together the crème fraîche and lemon, and reserve chilled until assembly.

TO SERVE

- 6 pickled, salt-cured, or smoked herring fillets
  vegetable oil or olive oil, as needed
- 2 tablespoons (3 grams) fresh dill, finely chopped
  lemon juice and zest, as needed
- 1 slice dark rye bread, toasted, and crushed
- 12 marble potatoes, boiled and peeled
  fresh parsley leaves, as needed

1. Arrange a herring fillet on each plate and lightly brush with some of the oil. Sprinkle each fillet with chopped dill, crushed rye bread, lemon juice, and zest. Arrange a few of the drained slices of pickled onion around each fillet, followed by the charred onion, eggplant ikra, parsley leaves, and additional dill. Serve alongside the lemon crème fraîche and warm boiled potato.

American-Irish Oysters

This exercise pays homage to the lost, legendary oyster industry of New York City and to the immigrant dock workers (many of whom were Irish) who once worked the bustling international port.

Pro Notes and Tips

• Shucking an oyster like a pro takes practice. Using an oyster knife, hold the oyster flat side up and, with your hands protected in a thick towel, wedge the tip of the knife at the point where the shells attach. Slightly turn the knife to separate the shells. Hold the oyster upright to avoid spilling the flavorful liquid. Run the knife flat along the top shell to detach the oyster and again underneath. The oyster will easily slide out of the shell.

BRAISED ARTICHOKES

3   young artichokes, trimmed, and halved
1   cup (250 grams) water
    juice of 1 lemon
1   tablespoon (15 grams) olive oil
1   bay leaf
3   sprigs fresh thyme
    fine sea salt, to taste

1. Place the artichoke halves in a small saucepan along with the water, lemon juice, olive oil, bay leaf, thyme, and a pinch of salt.

2. Bring the pan to a simmer and continue to cook over low heat, stirring occasionally, until the artichokes are cooked through and tender. Allow the artichokes to cool in the cooking liquid.

3. Once cool, cut the artichokes into a small dice.

MUSHROOM DUXELLES

1¾ ounces (50 grams) slab bacon, diced
2   large white button mushrooms (about 60 grams), finely diced
    fine sea salt, to taste
1   teaspoon (½ gram) fresh thyme, chopped
½ teaspoon red wine vinegar

1. Place diced bacon in a small saucepan and begin to render over low heat, stirring occasionally. Cook until bacon is lightly browned and crispy. Remove from the pan and reserve.

 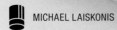

2. Add the diced mushrooms to the pan containing the rendered bacon fat, and begin to sweat over low heat, adding a pinch of salt and the chopped thyme.

3. Continue cooking until the mushrooms have just begun to brown and all of their moisture has cooked off. Remove from the heat and stir in the vinegar. Allow to cool.

VINAIGRETTE

⅛ teaspoon (½ gram) dry mustard powder
½ teaspoon (2 grams) ginger, peeled, and finely minced
2 teaspoon (10 grams) red wine vinegar
2 tablespoons (25 grams) vegetable oil
½ teaspoon (3 grams) Worcestershire sauce
fine sea salt, to taste
freshly ground black pepper, to taste

1. Combine all of the ingredients for the vinaigrette in a small mixing bowl and whisk until combined.

TO SERVE

12 small oysters
lime wedges, as needed
cilantro leaves, as needed

1. Clean and shuck the oysters, discarding the upper, flat half of the shell. Carefully loosen the oyster from the other half of the shell, avoiding any loss of the oyster "liquor."

2. Arrange each oyster on a bed of crushed ice or salt.

3. Spoon onto each oyster a few pieces of the artichoke, followed by a small spoonful of the duxelles, followed by a few pieces of rendered bacon. Spoon a bit of the vinaigrette over the top of each and finish with a leaf of cilantro. Add a few drops of fresh lime juice onto each oyster, or serve the lime wedges on the side. Serve immediately.

Greek Feta Burger

Cauliflower, eggplant fennel, and fava beans are not your usual suspects for a veggie burger, but maybe they should be. Favas make a solid base for the patty, and cabbage lends a very pleasing crunch. Fresh basil and chili sauce really bring the whole thing to life.

SURPRISE   PLEASANTNESS   SYNERGY

Pro Tips and Notes

- After forming the patties, refrigerating them for 20 to 30 minutes can make them easier to cook. If you are still having trouble with the patties holding together, gently coat them in flour before adding to the pan.

PATTY

- ½ cup (70 grams) fennel, minced
- 2 cups (200 grams) cauliflower, chopped
  pinch ground cinnamon
- 2 teaspoons (6 grams) dried oregano
- ½ teaspoon (2 grams) seasoning mix
- 2 15-ounce cans cooked fava beans, drained
- ½ cup (30 grams) bread crumbs
- 1 egg, beaten
- 1 cup (150 grams) feta
  vegetable oil, as needed

1. Briefly sauté the fennel. Add the cauliflower, and continue cooking until tender. As the vegetables cook, season with the cinnamon, seasoning mix, and oregano. Remove from the heat and set aside to cool.

2. Combine the cooked vegetables and drained fava beans in the bowl of a food processor. Purée until smooth. Then, transfer the mixture to a bowl and incorporate the bread crumbs, egg, and feta.

3. Form the patties and pan fry, cooking until golden brown on each side. Drain on paper towels before serving.

SPREAD

- 1 cup (250 grams) roasted eggplant
- ½ teaspoon (2 grams) fresh oregano leaves
- ½ teaspoon (2 grams) Sriracha
  vegetable oil, as needed

1. Place the eggplant on a baking sheet and pierce through the skin with a paring knife in a few spots. Roast at 350°F (175°C) until completely tender, about 45 minutes. Cut the eggplant in half and scoop the tender flesh from inside. Set it aside in a colander to drain briefly.

2. Heat a thin layer of oil in a sauté pan. Add the oregano leaves to the hot oil and cook until crisped.

3. Combine the drained eggplant, oregano leaves, the oil they were cooked in, and Sriracha in a bowl. Mix well to form a purée.

SLAW

- 2 cups (180 grams) cabbage, shredded
- 1 teaspoon (4 grams) Tabasco
- 2 teaspoons (6 grams) kosher salt
- 2 cups (80 grams) basil leaves
- ½ cup (120 grams) prepared mayonnaise

1. Combine the cabbage, Tabasco, and salt. Mix well, squeezing the cabbage to help it wilt. Set it aside for 20 minutes to soften.

2. Combine the basil leaves and mayonnaise in a blender and process until smooth.

3. Squeeze the cabbage to remove any excess moisture. Toss the cabbage with just enough of the basil mayonnaise to coat.

TO SERVE

1. Spread some of the spicy eggplant purée on the bottom of a bun. Top with the fava bean patty, then the cabbage slaw, and the bun top.

Korean Noodle Soup

There may not be much surprising about this dish, but the flavors are outstanding. I took the idea of kimchi and made it into a fresh aromatic base for the noodles, sautéing cabbage with ginger, radish, and chile. This dish can easily be made vegetarian by using vegetable broth and omitting the Chinese sausage.

CHEF WATSON SAYS

SURPRISE   PLEASANTNESS   SYNERGY

Pro Notes and Tips

• As with many soups, a good flavorful broth is the key here. Any smoked meats work well for developing flavor; you can use turkey wings or neck, smoked ham hocks—even bacon—as long as it's lower in fat.

• A pressure cooker allows you to make a very clean broth quickly; without one, gently simmer the broth ingredients together on the stove top for 4 hours.

PORK BROTH

2½ pounds (1,200 grams) smoked pork bones
4 cups (500 grams) mirepoix (chopped carrots, onions, celery)
1 cup (50 grams) dried mushrooms
1 head garlic, halved
1 piece kombu (about 40 grams), cut 6-inch (15-centimer) square
3 quarts (3,000 grams) water
1 cup (370 grams) soy sauce

1. Combine all the ingredients in a pressure cooker and bring to a simmer on top of the stove. Place the lid on the pot and bring to high pressure (15 psi) and cook for 90 minutes.

2. Dissipate the pressure in the pot to release the lid and strain the broth. Skim any fat from the surface and reserve the broth for soup. The broth will keep, frozen, for 6 months.

NOODLES

2 tablespoons (28 grams) sesame oil
2 tablespoons (18 grams) fresh ginger, sliced
1½ tablespoons (15 grams) garlic, chopped
1 teaspoon (2.5 grams) Korean red pepper flakes
½ cup (75 grams) Chinese sausage, sliced
1 cup (115 grams) daikon radishes, julienned
2 cups (160 grams) cabbage, thinly sliced
2 quarts (2,000 grams) pork or vegetable broth
2 cups (250 grams) lo mein noodles

1. Heat sesame oil in a sauce pot. Add the ginger and garlic, sautéing until very aromatic (about 2 minutes). Add red pepper flakes and sausage, and cook 1 minute more.

2. Stir in the radishes and cabbage, and continue cooking until just wilted. Add the broth and bring the mixture to a simmer. Simmer 10 minutes or until the cabbage is just tender (not completely soft). Stir in the noodles. Continue cooking until the noodles are tender.

TO SERVE

- ¼ cup (45 grams) radishes, thinly sliced
- ½ cup (20 grams) spinach, thinly sliced
- ½ cup (20 grams) daikon radish sprouts
  lotus chips, as needed (optional)
  sesame seeds, as needed

1. Spoon the noodles and reserved broth into bowls. Top with some of the raw radish slices, spinach, and sprouts. Add a few slices of the reserved meat from noodles, if desired, and sesame seeds.

American Kung Pao Chicken

This dish is an ode to the culture of Chinatown, further filtering this now largely Westernized dish through Watson's take on American cuisine. Challenging ingredients such as beets, cantaloupe, dates, and maple contributed a sweetness that needed to be carefully balanced. Unconventional herbs (at least from an Asian perspective), like rosemary and sage, provide an interesting underlying complexity.

CHEF WATSON SAYS

SURPRISE   PLEASANTNESS   SYNERGY

Pro Notes and Tips

- To considerably shorten the process of making this dish, substitute quicker-cooking chicken breast and pork tenderloin, preparing the proteins à la minute for the final assembly.

- The long pepper is more aromatic than conventional black pepper, but it can be replaced with whole black peppercorns in the brine and braising liquid.

Brine

- 3 tablespoons (45 grams) maple syrup
- 1-2 Thai chili peppers, split in half lengthwise
- 2 sprigs fresh rosemary
- 4 leaves fresh sage
- 2 pieces long pepper
- ¼ cup (40 grams) kosher salt
- 2 cups (450 grams) water
- 1 pound (450 grams) pork belly

1. Combine the maple, peppers, herbs, long pepper, salt, and water in a small saucepan and bring to a boil, stirring to dissolve salt. Remove from heat and cool completely.

2. Combine the pork belly and the brine in a container just large enough to hold the pork belly submerged. Cover and refrigerate for 8 to 12 hours.

Braise

- 2 cups (450 grams) water or chicken stock
- 1 Thai chili pepper, split in half lengthwise
- 1 sprig fresh rosemary
- 2 leaves fresh sage
- 1 piece long pepper

1. Remove the pork from the brine and discard the liquid. Rinse the pork belly under cold water to reduce excess saltiness. Gently dry the belly with paper towel.

2. Combine the pork belly and remaining ingredients in a shallow baking dish or ovenproof pan with a tight-fitting lid. Ensure that the pork belly is mostly submerged, adding additional liquid if necessary.

3. On the stove top, gently bring the pan to a simmer. Remove from heat, place the lid onto the pan (or wrap tightly with aluminum foil), place in an oven preheated to 275°F (135°C) and slowly braise for 4 to 5 hours.

4. Remove the pan from the oven and allow the pork belly to cool to room temperature in the braising liquid. Before transferring to the refrigerator, the texture and appearance can be improved by gently pressing the pork belly. To do so, loosely cover the pan with the pork belly and liquid, placing a second pan on top to gently compress. The cooked pork belly can be reserved, chilled, for up to 4 days.

CHICKEN THIGHS

3 chicken boneless thighs (about 450 grams), cut into bite-sized pieces
   fine sea salt, to taste
1 tablespoon (7 grams) tapioca starch
   vegetable oil, as needed

1. Arrange the cut pieces of chicken thigh on a plate, season with salt, and lightly dust with tapioca starch.

2. In a large sauté pan, heat a spoonful of oil over medium-high heat. Add the chicken and brown thoroughly on all sides. Remove from the heat, drain any excess fat, and add ½ cup (120 grams) defatted pork belly braising liquid.

3. Return to medium-low heat and continue cooking the chicken until the liquid has reduced by about half. Remove from the heat, cool, and reserve both the chicken and the remaining liquid.

JASMINE RICE

2½ cups (450 grams) water
  1 teaspoon (5 grams) fine sea salt
1½ cups (275 grams) jasmine rice

1. Place the water and salt in a medium-size saucepan with a tight-fitting lid; bring to a boil.

2. Stir in the rice, reduce the heat to low, and cover. Cook for 10 to 12 minutes and remove from the heat. Allow to stand covered for an additional 4 minutes.

3. Gently fluff the rice with a fork before serving.

TO SERVE

2 teaspoons (10 grams) vegetable oil
2 cups (about 6 ounces) fresh snow peas, trimmed
1 small beet, peeled, diced, and boiled until tender (reserve 2 tablespoons/30 grams of the cooking liquid)
1 ear sweet corn (about ½ cup), shucked, kernels removed from the cob
1 tablespoon (5 grams) poppy seeds
1 fresh Thai chili pepper, thinly sliced
¼ cup (30 grams) pitted dates, coarsely chopped
½ cup (50 grams) cucumber, thinly sliced and cut into wedges
1 teaspoon (2 grams) tapioca starch
2 teaspoons (10 grams) soy sauce
¼ cup (45 grams) cantaloupe melon, scooped into small balls

1. Heat the oil in a large wok or sauté pan over high heat and add the pieces of braised pork belly (trimmed of excess fat and sliced into bite-sized pieces), cooking until nicely browned. If desired, drain any excess rendered pork fat from the pan.

2. Add the previously cooked chicken thighs, tossing to reheat, followed immediately by the snow peas. Add the cooked beets, corn, poppy seeds, chili pepper, and dates, tossing to combine.

3. Meanwhile, combine the reserved braising liquid, beet liquid, and tapioca starch, and add the mixture to the pan, allowing the liquid to reduce slightly and thicken (coating the meat and vegetables). Add soy sauce, to taste.

4. Remove from heat and serve immediately alongside the rice, finishing with the cantaloupe melon balls.

Southern Fried Chicken

Soul food staples like black-eyed peas, chicken, and bright dried spices are the expected ingredients. Aromatic lime leaf, licorice, and tahini are anything but. I decided to make a nod to a classic preparation originating in Harlem—chicken and waffles—along with a well-loved ethnic street food: falafel!

CHEF WATSON SAYS

SURPRISE   PLEASANTNESS   SYNERGY

Pro Notes and Tips

- If you don't have time to soak your beans overnight, place the dried beans in a sauce pot and cover with cold water by 3 to 4 inches. Bring the pot to a boil, remove from heat and cover with a lid. Set aside to soak for 1 hour. Drain and rinse the beans and they are ready to use.

BLACK-EYED PEA FAL-WAFFLE

- 2 cups (335 grams) dried black-eyed peas, soaked overnight
- ½ cup (80 grams) onion, minced
- 1 tablespoon (20 grams) garlic, chopped
- 1 cup (30 grams) chives, chopped
- 2 teaspoons (8 grams) baking powder
- 1 egg
- 2 tablespoons (15 grams) all purpose flour
  vegetable oil, as needed

1. Combine the peas, onion, garlic, and chives in a food processor and purée. The mixture will not become perfectly smooth. Transfer to a bowl and mix in the baking powder, egg, and flour. Refrigerate for 30 minutes prior to cooking.

2. Drop 2 tablespoon-sized spoonfuls of batter into a hot, oiled waffle maker. Cook 6 minutes and remove (or deep-fry the mixture in oil at 350°F [175°C]).

TAHINI SAUCE

- 2 tablespoons (30 grams) tahini paste
- 1 tablespoon (14 grams) dark soy sauce
- ¼ cup (60 grams) yogurt
  Sriracha hot sauce, as needed
  water, as needed

1. Combine all of the ingredients in a bowl and mix well. Adjust consistency with water as needed.

SLAW

- ½ cup (45 grams) butternut squash, julienned or shredded
- 1 cup (90 grams) fennel, shaved
- ½ cup (45 grams) cucumber, julienned or shredded

1. Combine the vegetables in a bowl and season with salt. Dress with 2 tablespoons (30 grams) of the tahini sauce.

CHICKEN

- 8 boneless, skinless chicken thighs
  kosher salt, to taste
  smoked serrano pepper, to taste
- 1 cup (250 grams) buttermilk or low-fat milk
- 2 tablespoons (12 grams) aromatic lime leaf, sliced

2   cups (250 grams) all purpose flour
3   tablespoon (24 grams) kosher salt
2   tablespoons (18 grams) onion powder
½   teaspoon (2 grams) ground licorice root (optional)
    vegetable oil, as needed

1. Season the chicken generously with the salt and smoked pepper. Place in a bowl, add the buttermilk, and toss to coat. Refrigerate 2 hours up to overnight.

2. Combine the flour, salt, and onion powder, and mix well. Drain the chicken and add to the flour, then toss well to coat. Let the chicken rest in the flour for 5 minutes.

3. Optional step: Mix 2 tablespoons kosher salt and ground licorice root, reserve separately.

4. Heat a pot of oil to 325°F (160°C). Pat any excess flour from the chicken and cook in the oil until golden brown and a thermometer inserted into the meat registers 155°F (68°C) (about 8 minutes).

5. Rest on a rack and season immediately with the licorice salt or plain kosher salt.

Polish-Ukrainian Duck

There are several flavors to juggle in this Eastern European-inspired dish, and an autumnal stew seemed the most appropriate way to bring these ingredients together. Though duck is the key ingredient, the rich beef shank could easily overtake the dish. To provide balance I chose to confit the legs of the duck ensuring its starring role.

Pro Notes and Tips

- Confit, a French tradition of lightly curing, then slow-cooking meats in fat, originated as a means of preservation.

- The duck legs could also be braised alongside the beef shank, which would further add flavor to the braising liquid and the resulting sauce.

- Beef short ribs can be substituted for the shank.

BRAISED BEEF SHANK

      unsalted butter, as needed
    1 piece crosscut beef shank (900 grams)
      fine sea salt, to taste
  2-3 cups (450 to 700 grams) chicken stock, divided
    2 pieces whole cloves
    4 pieces whole juniper berries
    1 teaspoon (1.5 grams) caraway seeds
    2 teaspoons (2 grams) whole white peppercorns
    8 whole roasted chestnuts, peeled

1. Preheat a large sauté pan over medium heat and add a spoonful of butter.

2. Season the beef shank with salt and place in the hot pan. Thoroughly brown on all sides; remove the shank from the pan and discard excess fat. Deglaze the pan with 2 cups of the chicken stock and bring to a boil.

3. Combine beef shank, spices, and hot chicken stock in a shallow baking dish with a tight-fitting lid; ensure that the shank is mostly submerged, adding additional stock as necessary. Place the lid onto the pan (or wrap tightly with aluminum foil) and place in an oven preheated to 275°F (135°C), and slowly braise for 4 to 5 hours.

4. Remove the pan from the oven and allow the beef shank to cool to room temperature in the braising liquid.

5. When cool, defat and strain the braising liquid (reserve the chestnuts for the final assembly). Place the liquid in a small saucepan and bring to a simmer. Gently reduce the cooking liquid by roughly half. Meanwhile, pick the meat from the shanks and slice into bite-sized pieces, discarding excess fat and connective tissue.

DUCK CONFIT

  2½ tablespoons (50 grams) kosher salt
    2 pieces juniper berries, crushed
    1 teaspoon (1.5 grams) caraway seeds
    ½ teaspoon (0.5 gram) freshly ground white pepper
    2 duck legs
    2 cups (400 grams) duck fat

1. Combine the salt, crushed juniper berries, caraway seeds, and white pepper in a small bowl. Sprinkle the salt mixture on both sides of the duck legs and place in a shallow tray. Cover the duck legs and refrigerate for 8 to 12 hours.

2. Remove the duck legs and rinse away excess salt and spices. Pat dry with a paper towel and cover before bringing to room temperature.

3. In a small lidded pan or ovenproof dish, gently heat the duck fat to 180°F (82°C). Place the duck legs into the fat, ensuring that they are completely submerged. Cover and cook the confit over low heat for about 3 hours (or place the pan in an oven preheated to 250°F/120°C).

4. Remove from the heat and cool slowly at room temperature before transferring to the refrigerator to cool completely. Once cool, carefully trim the meat from the bones, keeping the skin intact and portioning into bite-sized pieces.

TO SERVE

  1 small green pepper (about 100 grams), seeded, and diced

  1 tablespoon (15 grams) red wine vinegar

  2 teaspoons (10 grams) honey

20 small marble or fingerling potatoes (450 grams), boiled

    fine sea salt, to taste

    freshly ground white pepper, to taste

  2 teaspoons (10 grams) unsalted butter

  3 cups (about 90 grams) loosely packed young spinach

  1 small Granny Smith apple, peeled, cored, and diced

  2 tablespoons (3 grams) fresh dill, finely chopped

1. Preheat a large sauté pan over medium low heat, and place the portioned duck leg confit into the pan skin side down. Gently brown the skin and remove from the pan.

2. Add the diced green pepper and cook for about 2 minutes, or just until softened.

3. Drain any excess fat from the pan and add the red wine vinegar, followed by the honey and reduced braising liquid. Add the portioned beef shank, duck confit, green peppers, potatoes, and chestnuts. Gently simmer to heat through. Adjust the seasoning with additional salt and pepper as necessary.

4. Meanwhile, heat the butter in a second sauté pan over medium heat and add the spinach. Season to taste and quickly stir the spinach until lightly wilted. Remove from heat and add to the first pan.

5. To serve, divide contents of the pan among 4 bowls, along with some of the braising liquid. Top each with some of the raw diced apple and a sprinkle of fresh dill.

Dominican Coconut Cake

In looking to create a cake inspired by tres leches, Watson suggested an intriguing Caribbean twist with the addition of the fiery habañero. The mild and sweet coconut—used in the soaking liquid, ice cream, and caramel sauce—provides just the right bridge between the spicy and fruity flavors.

CHEF WATSON SAYS

SURPRISE   PLEASANTNESS   SYNERGY

Pro Notes and Tips

- The light-as-air yogurt sponge is a playful component, prepared using a foam siphon and quickly cooked in a microwave.

- Lacking the necessary equipment, the tart edge of the yogurt could easily replace the cream in the soaking liquid.

ALMOND CORNMEAL CAKE

¼ cup plus 2 tablespoons (100 grams) almond paste
2 eggs (about 100 grams)
1 tablespoon (15 grams) honey
  pinch (1 gram) fine sea salt
2 tablespoons (15 grams) all purpose flour
1½ tablespoons (15 grams) cornmeal
  pinch cayenne pepper
¼ cup (55 grams) unsalted butter, melted

1. Place the almond paste in the bowl of an electric stand mixer fitted with the paddle attachment and beat the almond paste until softened.

2. Gradually incorporate the whole eggs, one at a time, scraping the bowl after each addition. Then add the honey, followed by the salt.

3. Add the flour, cornmeal, and cayenne pepper, mixing just until incorporated, followed by the melted butter.

4. Transfer to a small parchment-lined baking pan 6- by 8-inches (15- by 20-centimeters). Place in an oven preheated to 320°F (160°C) for 12 to 15 minutes (or until an inserted pick removes clean). Allow to cool.

5. Carefully remove the cake from the pan by inverting onto a work surface. Trim the sides of the cake, cut into 6 long strips, and reserve for soaking.

SOAKING LIQUID

½ cup (120 grams) coconut milk
½ cup (120 grams) sweetened condensed milk
½ cup (110 grams) heavy cream (35% fat)
  pinch ground cinnamon

1. Combine the coconut milk, condensed milk, cream, and cinnamon in a small bowl and whisk to combine. Place the strips of almond cake into a shallow dish and add the soaking liquid. Cover and refrigerate for 1 to 2 hours.

COCONUT VANILLA ICE CREAM

1¼ cups (300 grams) whole milk
1½ cups (350 grams) heavy cream (35% fat)
1 vanilla bean, split, scraped
2 tablespoons (15 grams) nonfat dry milk powder
¾ cup plus 2 tablespoons (170 grams) granulated sugar
6 egg yolks (about 120 grams)
1½ cups (350 grams) coconut milk

1. Place the milk, cream, vanilla, and milk powder in a saucepan and bring to a boil, whisking occasionally.

2. Meanwhile, combine the sugar and egg yolks in a mixing bowl and whisk thoroughly.

3. Slowly temper the hot milk into the yolk mixture. Return to low heat and cook, stirring, until the mixture reaches 185°F (85°C).

4. Remove from heat and whisk in the coconut milk. Mix well with an immersion blender. Chill in an ice water bath. Allow mixture to steep for at least 12 hours in the refrigerator.

5. Process in an ice cream machine according to manufacturer's instructions; reserve ice cream in the freezer.

YOGURT MICRO SPONGE

¼ cup plus 2 tablespoons (90 grams) Greek-style yogurt
3 egg whites (about 100 grams)
¼ cup plus 1 tablespoon (75 grams) granulated sugar
3 tablespoons (20 grams) Wondra or all purpose flour
pinch fine sea salt

1. Combine all of the ingredients in a mixing bowl and whisk until well mixed. Pass through a fine mesh sieve.

2. Transfer the mixture to a 1-pint foam siphon and load two N_2O gas chargers, per manufacturer's instructions.

3. Dispense mixture into roughly six 8-ounce paper cups, into which a few holes are punched.

4. Place each cup in the microwave and cook on high for 35 to 40 seconds.

5. Remove cups from microwave, invert, and cool. Reserve.

COCONUT CARAMEL SAUCE

½ cup plus 1 tablespoon (115 grams) granulated sugar
3 tablespoons (45 grams) water
¼ teaspoon (2 grams) lemon juice
2 teaspoons (10 grams) glucose or light corn syrup
¼ cup (60 grams) heavy cream (35% fat)
¼ cup (60 grams) coconut milk
1 tablespoon (15 grams) unsalted butter

1. Combine the sugar, water, lemon, and corn syrup in a heavy saucepan. Over medium heat, without stirring, cook the mixture to a dark amber color. Meanwhile, heat the cream and coconut milk until warm.

2. Remove the caramelized sugar from heat and deglaze with the cream. Return to a low heat to completely dissolve the sugar, stirring if necessary.

3. Remove from heat and whisk the butter into the caramel. Allow to cool, then transfer to a squeeze bottle.

WHITE WINE HABAÑERO CARAMEL

½ cup (100 grams) granulated sugar
water, as needed
1 cup (225 grams) white wine
1 thin slice habañero pepper (about 2 grams)

1. Combine the sugar and water just to cover in a small saucepan. Cook without stirring, to a light amber color.

2. Remove from the heat and slowly add the wine. Return to the heat, add the habañero, and bring to a gentle simmer. Continue to cook to 221°F (105°C). Allow to cool, remove the habañero, and transfer to a squeeze bottle.

ROASTED BANANA

- 2 bananas (about 200 grams), peeled
- 2 tablespoons (30 grams) unsalted butter, melted
- 2 tablespoons (25 grams) light brown sugar

1. Prepare small balls of the banana by portioning with a melon baller (or chop into small, uniform pieces).

2. In a small bowl, combine the melted butter and brown sugar. Add the banana and toss to coat. Arrange the banana pieces in a shallow ovenproof dish or baking sheet. Roast bananas in a preheated 350°F (175°C) oven for 4 to 6 minutes (or until slightly caramelized). Remove from the oven and reserve, keeping warm for assembly.

TO SERVE

- ½ cup (100 grams) diced mango
     zest of 1 lime, finely grated
     ground cinnamon, as needed for dusting

1. Remove the strips of almond cake from the soaking liquid and place onto each serving plate. Spoon some of the remaining soaking liquid over the cake, if desired.

2. Carefully remove the small pieces of the yogurt sponge from the cups and place them randomly around the cake. Then add pieces of the roasted banana and diced mango.

3. Place several drops of the coconut caramel and white wine caramel around the plate. Place a scoop of the ice cream onto the cake. Finish with a sprinkle of lime zest and a light dusting of cinnamon.

Italian Pumpkin Cheesecake

I debated for a long time whether this cheesecake should be sweet or savory. With spices like cumin and paprika, plus mushrooms, there were plenty of signs to point it in the savory direction. In the end, I opted to make it sweet. Making a rich mushroom broth scented with ginger and cooking it down to a glaze with brown sugar resulted in a deep, molasses-like flavor.

CHEF WATSON SAYS

SURPRISE   PLEASANTNESS   SYNERGY

Pro Notes and Tips

• Methocel F50, which is made from cellulose (plant cell walls), is the ultimate stabilizer. It allows any low-fat liquid mixture to whip into a nice foam. It cannot be over-whipped, holds its shape well, and can be dried to make meringues. If you do not have Methocel F50, simply fold the mushroom glaze into whipped cream to garnish the cake.

PUMPKIN PURÉE

- 2 tablespoons (28 grams) unsalted butter
- 2 tablespoons (16 grams) fresh ginger, chopped
- 3 cups (500 grams) pumpkin or butternut squash, cut into 1-inch (2½-centimeter) cubes
- 2 teaspoons (8 grams) paprika
- 2 teaspoons (8 grams) cumin seeds
- 2 teaspoons (6 grams) kosher salt
- 1 cup (225 grams) water

1. Melt the butter in a large sauté pan over medium heat. Add the ginger and sauté until aromatic, about 1 minute.

2. Add the pumpkin, paprika, cumin seeds, and salt. Continue cooking briefly on the stovetop.

3. Before the pumpkin browns, add the water and immediately cover the pan with a lid. Reduce the heat to low and cook, covered, until completely tender. Transfer the mixture to a blender and process until smooth.

PUMPKIN CHEESECAKE

- 1 cup (240 grams) ricotta cheese
- 4 ounces (115 grams) Neufchâtel cheese
- ½ cup (100 grams) sugar
- 1 teaspoon (3 grams) kosher salt
- 4 eggs
- 6 tablespoons (80 grams) butter
- 2 cups (140 grams) cracker crumbs

1. Combine 1 cup (240 grams) of the pumpkin purée, ricotta, Neufchâtel cheese, and sugar in the bowl of a food processor. Blend until smooth. Add the eggs and process again.

2. Lightly grease a 13- by 9-inch (33- by 23-centimeter) baking pan. Melt butter in a small pan, add the cracker crumbs, and mix well. Turn the cracker crumbs out into greased pan and press firmly into a single layer.

3. Pour the cheesecake batter over the crumbs and tilt the pan to get the batter into a flat, even layer. Bake in a 325°F (162°C) oven until just set (about 25 minutes). Cool completely before cutting.

MUSHROOM-GINGER WHIP MERINGUES

1 tablespoon (15 grams) butter
1 tablespoon (8 grams) ginger, chopped
2 cups (160) grams mushrooms, sliced
4 cups (900 grams) water
½ ounce (15 grams) dried mushrooms
2 tablespoons (30 grams) light brown sugar
1 cup (115 grams) skim milk
  0.3% xanthan gum by weight (weight x 0.003)
  1.0% Methocel F50 by weight (weight x 0.01)

1. Melt the butter in a sauce pot. Add the ginger and mushrooms, sauté until dry. Add the water, dried mushrooms, and sugar. Bring the mixture to a simmer and reduce by two-thirds. Strain into a clean bowl. Stir in the milk and weigh the combined liquid.

2. Transfer the mixture to a blender, add the xanthan gum and Methocel F50, and blend to dissolve. Move the liquid to the bowl of an electric mixer and whip until tripled in volume.

3. Divide the mixture in half. Place half of the foam in a piping bag and pipe into "kisses" (pointed droplets) on a nonstick baking sheet. Place in a 150°F (65°C) to dry.

TO SERVE

  shavings of white chocolate (optional)

1. Cut the cheesecake into 4- by 1-inch (10- by 2½-centimeter) bars. Place a spoonful of mushroom whipped cream in the center of a large plate. Place the cheesecake on top of the whip. Garnish with white chocolate shavings and mushroom meringues.

Turkish Yogurt Trifle

This dish, conceived as a dessert, was one of my earliest interactions with Watson. While the parameters were set to include enough basic ingredients to construct some form of pastry element (flour, dairy, egg, sweetener), the challenge arose when the output offered not plain, all purpose flour, but semolina and rice flour in its place.

CHEF WATSON SAYS

SURPRISE   PLEASANTNESS   SYNERGY

Pro Notes and Tips

- This yogurt panna cotta was formulated to be firm enough to hold its freestanding shape (I like to set the mixture in flexible silicone molds). If serving in a glass as a layered dessert, simply reduce the gelatin by 1 sheet to produce a softer texture.

SEMOLINA CAKE

- 2 eggs (about 100 grams)
  zest of 1 lemon, finely grated
- ½ cup (100 grams) granulated sugar
- 2 tablespoons (30 grams) honey
- ¼ teaspoon (0.5 gram) powdered ginger
- ¼ teaspoon (0.5 gram) cayenne pepper
- ¾ cup (125 grams) semolina
- 1 tablespoon (10 grams) brown rice flour
- ½ teaspoon (3 grams) fine sea salt
- 2 tablespoons (30 grams) unsalted butter, melted
- 2 tablespoons (30 grams) whole milk
- ¼ cup (35 grams) sesame seeds

1. In the bowl of an electric stand mixer fitted with the whip attachment, combine the eggs, lemon zest, sugar, and honey. Whip the mixture on medium speed for 4 minutes (or until lightened).

2. Gently fold the ginger, cayenne, semolina, rice flour, and salt into the egg mixture, followed by the melted butter and milk. Allow the batter to rest for 20 minutes.

3. Transfer the batter to a parchment-lined 8-inch (20-centimeter) baking dish. Sprinkle the sesame seeds on top of the batter and place in a preheated 320°F (160°C) oven and bake for 25 to 30 minutes (or until an inserted pick removes clean). Remove from the oven and thoroughly cool.

4. When cool, slice or tear the cake into bite-sized pieces and reserve for assembly.

 SERVES 6

 50 MINUTES, PLUS BAKING AND FREEZING

 MICHAEL LAISKONIS

YOGURT PANNA COTTA

¾ cup (175 grams) heavy cream (35% fat)

¼ cup plus 2 tablespoons (75 grams) granulated sugar
zest of 1 lemon

3 leaves sheet gelatin, bloomed in cold water and drained

½ cup (125 grams) plain whole-milk Greek-style yogurt

1. In a saucepan, combine the cream, sugar, and zest, gently warming over medium heat.

2. Remove from heat and add the gelatin, stirring until dissolved. Temper into the milk and yogurt and strain through a fine-mesh sieve. Drop into your desired mold or silicone form and refrigerate. Allow 2 hours to set.

RED WINE CARAMEL

½ cup (100 grams) granulated sugar
water, as needed

1 cup (225 grams) red wine

1. Combine sugar and water to cover in a small saucepan. Carefully cook, without stirring, to a light amber color.

2. Remove from the heat and slowly add the wine. Return to the heat and bring to a gentle simmer. Continue to cook to 221°F (105°C). Allow to cool and transfer to a squeeze bottle.

SLOW-ROASTED RED FRUITS

1 cup (200 grams) strawberries, rinsed, hulled, and sliced crosswise

1 cup (200 grams) cherries, rinsed, pitted, and halved

2 teaspoons (10 grams) lemon juice

2 tablespoons (25 grams) granulated sugar

1. Combine all of the ingredients in a small mixing bowl and toss to combine.

2. Spread the fruit into a baking dish and place in a 275°F (135°C) oven and roast until just softened (10 to 12 minutes). Remove from the oven and cool.

TO SERVE

1. Unmold the frozen panna cotta and place onto serving plates. Allow it to temper until softened (20 to 30 minutes).

2. Around each panna cotta, arrange pieces of the semolina cake and the roasted fruit. Finish with several drops of the red wine caramel.

New Amsterdam Apple Pudding

Based on Watson's output, bread pudding would have been the obvious route to go here. Instead, I chose an unexpected path, making caramelized apples into a traditional stirred pudding.

CHEF WATSON SAYS

SURPRISE   PLEASANTNESS   SYNERGY

Pro Notes and Tips

- This dessert looks great unmolded. To keep a nice shape to the pudding, freeze in cups or in a flexible mold. Remove them from the molds while still frozen and thaw on a plate.

- If you choose to serve this dessert in cups, you can omit the gelatin from the recipe.

CURRIED RAISIN COULIS

- ¾ cup (150 grams) raisins
- 1¾ fluid ounces (400 grams) white wine
- 1 tablespoon (8 grams) curry powder
- 1 teaspoon (3 grams) dry mustard

1. Combine raisins, white wine, curry powder, and mustard. Simmer gently until wine is reduced by three-fourths. Transfer to a blender and process until smooth.

APPLE PUDDING

- 2 tablespoons (28 grams) butter
- 4 apples (about 590 grams), peeled, and chopped
- ½ cup (100 grams) brown sugar
- ¼ cup (60 grams) rye whiskey
- 1 cup (225 grams) heavy cream
- 1 cup (225 grams) milk
- 1 teaspoon (3 grams) powdered gelatin
- 2 tablespoons (28 grams) water
- 1 egg
- 2 egg yolks

1. Melt butter in a large sauté pan over high heat. When it begins to brown slightly, add the apples and brown sugar. Sauté until completely dry and softened (about 5 minutes). Deglaze with rye whiskey. Add milk and cream, and bring the mixture to a simmer.

2. Transfer to a blender and process until smooth. Strain into a clean pot.

3. Sprinkle the gelatin over the water and allow 2 to 3 minutes to soften. Whisk the softened gelatin, egg, and egg yolks into the apple purée. Stir the mixture gently, over a low flame, until thickened. Transfer to cups and refrigerate to set.

BUTTERMILK WHITE CHOCOLATE MOUSSE

- 1 cup (130 grams) white chocolate
  zest of ½ orange
- ½ cup (115 grams) buttermilk, room temperature
- 1 cup (225 grams) heavy cream, whipped to stiff peaks

1. Combine the chocolate and orange zest in a heat-proof bowl. Set the bowl over a pot of simmering water to melt (double-boiler method).

2. Remove from heat and whisk in the buttermilk. Fold in the whipped cream and refrigerate.

RYE WALNUT CRUMBLE

2	tablespoons (28 grams) butter
½	cup (15 grams) rye bread, torn into small pieces
¼	cup (20 grams) walnuts, chopped
1	teaspoon (3 grams) anise seeds
	pinch kosher salt

1. Melt the butter over medium heat in a large sauté pan. Add the bread and sauté 1 minute. Add the walnuts and cook 1 minute more. When the bread begins to brown, add the anise seeds and a pinch of salt. Drain immediately on paper towels and reserve.

TO SERVE

1. Spread some of the curried raisin coulis across the base of each plate. Unmold the pudding onto the coulis and garnish with some of the crumble and a spoonful of the chocolate mousse.

7 Cognitive Cocktails

Anthony Caporale, a longtime mixologist, is the Director of Beverage Studies at the Institute of Culinary Education. When he began working with Watson, he was drawn to the system's "surprise" algorithm. How could he work with it to create the most unexpected cocktails?

He came up with a seemingly impossible idea. He would ask Watson to build drinks around proteins. These would be savory cocktails—four of them— each containing one of the typical proteins found (in one form or another) on restaurant menus: chicken, fish, beef, and pork.

The results span an incredible range of flavors. Some, like the Plum Pancetta Cider, blend elements of meat and fruit. Others, such as the Shrimp Cocktail, unite an appetizer with a cocktail in a humorous twist. And while you may have enjoyed an Old Fashioned before, have you ever tried one made with chicken broth?

COGNITIVE COCKTAILS

Hoof-n-Honey Ale

Beer cocktails are some of the most popular drinks in the beverage world, but the addition of veal stock makes this drink a one-of-a-kind creation! Blending the time-tested combination of beer, beef, and Burgundy wine with the sweetness of peaches and honey, this drink is at once surprising and familiar.

CHEF WATSON SAYS

SURPRISE   PLEASANTNESS   SYNERGY

Pro Notes and Tips:

• For thicker foam, use an immersion blender.

• Any good pinot noir can be substituted for the Burgundy wine.

   SERVES 1   🕐 10 MINUTES   ANTHONY CAPORALE

HONEY SYRUP
    honey, as needed
    warm water, as needed

1. Combine equal parts honey and warm water, stirring until dissolved. Chill before using.

BURGUNDY FOAM
  4 ounces Burgundy wine
  1 egg white
  1 teaspoon confectioners sugar

1. Add all of the ingredients to a mixing tin and dry shake without ice until thickened.

TO SERVE
  4 ounces chilled India Pale Ale
  1 ounce veal stock
  2 slices peach
  1 small piece of grilled beef

1. In a mixing glass, add the India Pale Ale, ½ ounce honey syrup, and veal stock. Stir gently.

2. Pour into a coupe glass and float the peach slices, then layer 1 ounce of the Burgundy foam.

3. Garnish with grilled beef.

Plum Pancetta Cider

Using the fat-washing technique, this drink cleverly manages to bring the proven pairing of pork and apples to a cocktail. Pancetta-washed cider provides the base, while sake and lemon juice balance plum and palm sugar to create a flavor experience that complements food or stands on its own.

CHEF WATSON SAYS

SURPRISE   PLEASANTNESS   SYNERGY

Pro Notes and Tips:

- Be sure to allow the fat to cool, but not solidify, before adding it to the cider.

- When muddling, steady the glass with one hand while pushing down and twisting the muddler using the other hand.

PANCETTA-WASHED CIDER

¼ pound pancetta
8 ounces cider

1. Fry pancetta and reserve. Add cooled, rendered fat to the cider.

2. Stir gently and rest overnight. Chill to solidify fat and strain cider through a coffee filter.

PALM SUGAR SYRUP

sugar, as needed
warm water, as needed

1. Combine equal parts palm sugar and warm water. Stir to dissolve.

TO SERVE

1 ounce chilled rice wine
2 slices plum
4 ounces chilled pancetta-washed cider
1 strip cooked pancetta
1 orange peel
squeeze lemon wedge

1. In a mixing glass, muddle ½ ounce palm sugar syrup, the chilled rice wine, and the plum slices.

2. Half fill the glass with ice, then add 4 ounces of the chilled pancetta-washed cider and the squeeze of lemon. Stir gently.

3. Strain into a hurricane glass over fresh ice and garnish with a strip of fried pancetta and a long slice of orange peel.

The Shrimp Cocktail

You may have had shrimp cocktail, but you've never had the Shrimp Cocktail. This "appetini" (as Anthony calls his creation) delivers as both a drink and an appetizer, marrying the savory flavors of shrimp and bay leaf with the brightness of lemon juice, vermouth, and orange.

CHEF WATSON SAYS

SURPRISE   PLEASANTNESS   SYNERGY

Pro Notes and Tips:

- Much of a lemon's flavor comes from essential oils in the skin, so dropping the peel into the drink after juicing it allows the alcohol to dissolve those oils.

- You know you've shaken your cocktail to the correct temperature when frost forms on the outside of the mixing tin.

TO SERVE

2	ounces dry vermouth
¼	ounce Cointreau
	juice of ½ lemon, plus peel
2	bay leaves
2	butterflied Cajun-spiced grilled shrimp

1. In a mixing tin half filled with ice, add the dry vermouth, Cointreau, lemon juice and peel, and 1 bay leaf. Shake until the tin is frosted.

2. Strain into a martini glass lined with the shrimp and garnish with the remaining bay leaf.

 SERVES 1

 10 MINUTES

 ANTHONY CAPORALE

Corn in the Coop

This drink pushes a Bourbon Old Fashioned into entirely new territory by adding ginger, apple juice, and—most surprisingly—chicken stock. A hint of orange and lemongrass provides the perfect touch of citrus to balance the earthier flavors, producing a drink that refreshes as it satisfies.

CHEF WATSON SAYS

SURPRISE   PLEASANTNESS   SYNERGY

Pro Notes and Tips:

- Cut the orange peel with as little pith (white) as possible to avoid adding bitter oils to the drink.

- To express added flavor from the peel, hold it between both thumbs and forefingers with the orange zest side facing the drink, and squeeze it quickly to distribute the essential oils over the surface of the drink.

TO SERVE

1½	ounces bourbon
2	ounces apple juice
1	ounce chicken stock
2	slices ginger
1	stalk lemongrass
1	small piece grilled chicken
	orange peel, as needed

1. In a mixing glass half filled with ice, add all of the ingredients. Stir to chill thoroughly.

2. Strain into a rocks glass filled with fresh ice. Express an orange peel over the top. Garnish with expressed peel, a stalk of lemongrass, and grilled chicken.

Index

Index

Index

Index